Jörg-Michael Müller

THE
FORGOTTEN
ARTIST

William „Bill" Alexander

Imprint

Copyright: Jörg-Michael Müller
Title design and typesetting:
Kunstportal Hamburg,
Jörg-Michael Müller

Manufacturing and publishing:
BoD - Books on Demand, Norderstedt
ISBN: 9783758327209

"Life is a big, blank canvas,
and we fill it up ourselves with the magic of our lives.
Each of us comes to the canvas to create that one special
almighty painting. For some it is easy; for others,
it is not. For me, it has been a long journey."

William "Bill" Alexander, 1983 [1]

Originally this book was only planned in German language. However, I received several requests written in English as to whether I could translate this book into English, as there is obviously not a single comprehensive biography of William Alexander in the world. That generally sounded like a very good idea to me. However, I must point out that my English is just as improvable as William's was! Despite the greatest effort and care, you will definitely encounter typos and inelegant wording here that are not present in the German version. I ask that you treat this with indulgence and hope that you enjoy the exciting life story of William "Bill" Alexander.

Jörg-Michael Müller, 03. Januar 2024

Table of contents

About hidden springs in the fog and small strokes of luck

William "Bill" Alexander, the artist who was born in Berlin and emigrated to North America, developed the ingenious "Alexander painting technique" with which he was able to create complex oil paintings in a very short time. As a TV painter with his own show, he became famous throughout the country, and his painting technique is still used today by enthusiastic people around the world. All over the globe, countless painting teachers still earn their living with this technique, and the sale of the special paints and brushes was and still is a million-dollar business. However, William Alexander was forgotten after his death; hardly anyone in German-speaking countries knows him anyway. The worldwide fame for the ingenious "Alexander painting technique" went to someone else. His student and former employee Bob Ross. It is urgently overdue to remember this artist. He was a charming rascal and a filou who survived two world wars and traveled around North America and Canada as a traveling artist in his VW bus for decades, until he was discovered in the early 1970s and became a celebrated star. He dreamed of a better tomorrow, loved nature and people. Throughout his life he spoke out against greed and war. His life was winding, sometimes dramatic. Especially his last years, and his adventurous biography reads as excitingly as a novel.

When I first started researching William Alexander, it wasn't very difficult to put together information about him. There was a documentary[2] from 1983 about William and also an autobiography.[3] Many details were also learned by carefully watching the individual episodes of his TV show.[4] Today you can almost only find them on YouTube. But at a certain point the research suddenly stopped and there were no further sources available. From his childhood onwards, through his time as a Wehrmacht soldier, his life could be told, albeit incompletely. Much of the winding path to his breakthrough remains obscure. Until 1992, he was known to an audience of millions in North America through his TV shows; little is known about his private life. But then everything suddenly became completely quiet around him, and the last years of his life were completely in a fog. According to online sources, he is said to have lived in a difficult-to-access town called Powell River[5] until his death. But that is already wrong. Only the date of his death could be determined without any doubt, January 24, 1997. His burial place also raises questions. A source says he is in the cemetery in Powell River. However, other sources claim, he was buried in Port Alberni[6]. At the end, both are not true. His grave is not in either cemetery, and when I delved into the research it was completely unclear whether his grave could even be located. The more I dug, the more unanswered questions and inconsistencies emerged. In the end, this biography would have remained almost unsatisfactorily incomplete, if chance had not come to the rescue, so that I can now tell his entire dramatic life story.

As a matter of routine, I first wrote to all the cemeteries in question and asked for information as to whether the painter William Alexander was buried there. I received a response from Powell River within just a few hours. It was true, the person in question is not in their cemetery, a friendly employee of cemetery administration told me. But I received the address of a funeral home. Maybe, according to the lady, they could help me there. So I sent the undertaker my request, which was also answered after a few hours. I was informed that the person in question was not buried by the company, but the employee checked the central register and copied Mr. Alexander's death certificate for me. I could not believe my eyes. In Germany this would be absolutely impossible for data protection reasons, but in Canada the clocks seem to tick differently. This official document was extremely helpful, but the highlight of the whole thing was that the death certificate was signed by a relative of William Alexander, who was completely unknown to me until then. He had a daughter, that is documented. According to this document, there was also a foster son. Sometimes luck helps the brave, as I actually managed to locate this foster son somewhere in the depths of Canada. I explained my concerns to the 74-year-old and he was actually willing to answer all of my countless questions. We exchanged ideas for months, and without him it would not have been possible to tell the exciting life story of William "Bill" Alexander with all its facets.

04.01. 2024, Jörg-Michael Müller

A childhood full of deprivation in East Prussia

William Alexander's family (he was born with the name Wilhelm) lived in that time in sparsely populated East Prussia. At these days, when noble landowners such as the Counts of Dohna,[7] those of Finckenstein[8] or Döhnhoff[9] ruled there. Agriculture made them rich and powerful, and East Prussia was a bulging granary. The large and stately two-story manor houses still bear witness to the former wealth of the "blue-blooded people," as the simple rural people derisively called the rural and moneyed nobility. Of course, the common people, around three-quarters of whom worked in agriculture and were therefore directly dependent on the nobility, lived much more modestly. Their houses were small and one-story, they usually only had a simple clay floor, a small cooking area, a sparse oven, and they usually used sacks filled with straw to sleep on after a hard day. The Alexander family lived in a village called Rautenberg,[10] consisting of a collection of around three dozen small, mainly one-story houses. There was a small train station with a single track in the direction of Tilsit, which is around 40 kilometers away, a blacksmith, a hairdresser, a saddler, a small school, on the upper floor of which the teacher also lived. There was also a post office, a church and a small shop for the essentials: sugar, salt, pepper and flour. That was it already. There was no real doctor, there was no pharmacy, no cobbler and certainly no electricity. Electricity did not reach Rautenberg until 1927, and the generator that produced the electricity for the sparse street lighting was from then on looked after by the local blacksmith.There was an old police officer there, but it was a rough time with tough guys back then. And if there was a dispute between the neighbors, for example because one of them moved the boundary stone to the neighboring property a little in his favor, then they usually settled it directly among themselves. With your fists or with a shotgun. That's how it was back then. There wasn't much of a fuss about it. If someone in the village was „shot down," as William reported many years later, there would simply be one fewer of them there in the future.

Already in those days, modern agricultural techniques were being developed in East Prussia, which were partly responsible for the high agricultural yields. William's father, also called Wilhelm, worked as a construction manager at the time and implemented these techniques. At times, up to 200 workers were under his command and they built the most modern drainage systems and pumps to remove water from the moors[11] and thus gain new arable land. They also built paths and canals and cleaned the rivers. The mother, her name was Ida, born Pasanau, looked after her two-year-old son Paul and looked after the small house. They also had a modest piece of land leased to the local landlord, which they managed for their own use. They grew the bare necessities and kept a few cattle, chickens and geese. In addition to a few dogs, the Alexander family also owned an aging horse.

In the summer of 1914, the mother became pregnant with William. At the same time, the drama of the First World War was brewing on the world stage, at the end of which 17 million victims would be mourned. After the assassination attempt on the heir to the Austrian throne in Sarajevo on June 28, the German Reich promised Austria in July that it would stand by Austria's side, regardless of how Austria would react to the assassination attempt. Armed with this "blank check," Austria then declared war on Serbia, which, however, was supported by Russia. On July 30th, the Austrians and Russians were already at war. The German Reich then immediately declared war on Russia, France and England, and the madness began. The military leadership of the German Reich was well aware of the danger of a two-front war. And to prevent this, the so-called "Schlieffen Plan" was developed years before. This stipulated that through a rapid attack on France from the north and south, disregarding Belgian neutrality, France would be defeated so quickly that the army could then turn directly to the east, even before the Russian mobilization was complete. They were confident of victory in Berlin, but that was a mistake. Of course, the Alexander family knew nothing or very little about all of these plans. But people in East Prussia were worried because there were only a few troops on site to defend them. And contrary to imperial expectations, after just 14 days there were two tsarist armies in the country. Atrocities, escape and devastation were the result, but the Alexander family has so far been spared. However, the East Prussian nobility feared for their land and prosperity and turned directly to Kaiser Wilhelm II for help. They were then listened to by the Hohenzoller[12], and two corps were detached from the attacking army moving westward, which had not even reached the Marne, and marched eastward. Under Hindenburg and Ludendorff, one of the two tsarist armies was destroyed at the Battle of Tannenberg[13] and the second was pushed eastwards. But this army still controlled large parts of East Prussia. In February 1915, in the "Winter Battle of Masuria,"[14] the German attack on the remaining second tsarist army took place. Now the Alexander family also had to flee quickly to protect life and limb. Since the father had long been enlisted as a soldier and fought, he was wounded three times during the war, and his son William would surpass this number in the next war - that's how it was the grandfather riding the horse on a wet, cold and rainy morning in February hastily hitched up to the cart, while the heavily pregnant mother gathered the essentials. In a long refugee trek they set off on the arduous and dangerous journey towards Berlin, where on April 2nd, after a safe arrival, William Alexander saw the electric light of this world, safe and sound. Incidentally, William Alexander had never visited his birthplace, Berlin, in his life.

William later spoke about his grandfather with a wink. At that time he was employed as a rural postman and usually traveled from place to place in a carriage for days at a time, and it was only long years after the war that the family found out that the grandfather was quite busy, because he had a girlfriend in almost every town on his route. But that doesn't really matter here, so we'll just skip it.

After the war, the Alexander family returned to Rautenberg and their son Heinrich was born. The land was plowed by bombs and shells, and all the houses were destroyed. And still the half-decayed bodies of soldiers lay where they once died, and the entire land lay under a foul-smelling blanket of decay. Charred weapon parts and equipment, half-rusted grenades and ammunition lay everywhere. The father had to take out a loan to build a new house. But for the children it was a huge, exciting adventure playground, albeit a smelly one. William Alexander later reported that they initially thought it would be a good idea to remove the soldiers' boots from the corpses so that they could have shoes of their own or sell them. But the smell inside the shoes made her quickly throw that idea overboard. Instead, they turned their attention to the grenades lying around. They were already half rusted and the children threw stones at them to make them explode. It quickly became a common saying to "let it rip for once." Many of the children lost an arm, an eye or even their entire life.

The East Prussian winters were long and harsh, it quickly became freezing cold and a lot of snow fell. Everyone in the family had to pitch in and help to make ends meet. Young William was very adept at hunting rabbits. The mountain hares had such wonderfully soft fur that could be used to make warm clothing. However, one winter was so bitterly cold that the Alexander family had to kill their old sheepdog Hector to get his fur. The family's other dogs soon followed. As I said, it was a tough time and we can hardly imagine it today. William walked almost the entire year fishing with his brothers. For them it was fun, but also an addition to their menu. They caught perch and carp. And the catfish, which he called mudfish and which the children loved to eat raw. He enjoyed fishing so much that his dream job in those days was that of a fish warden. This used to be a respected position, you were in the civil service and made sure that the water was intact, there was no pollution, and you were always in the fresh air. That meant freedom for William. Unfortunately, you had to study and take exams for this. But the Alexander family couldn't afford all of this. Things improved over the years as his father went back to work as a construction manager. And the piece of land was now back diligently cultivated for their own use, and they also had a few cows and chickens again. William was particularly good at keeping bees. He loved her sweet honey. In his memoirs, William later wrote how the children enjoyed sitting together as a family, singing and playing music together. One of the brothers played the harmonica and William played the fiddle. When spring came and it got warmer, the boys strolled through nature. Even as a child, William loved the fields, pastures and forests around him, through which he loved to run. However, the forests belonged to the East Prussian rural nobility, and they didn't like villagers staying there. If the "blue bloods" caught a boy, they quickly got a few hits. But that hadn't stopped anyone from going into the woods again and again. The children attended the small school in town. The girls sat in front and the boys sat behind them. And her teacher, called "Greybeard," taught her everything that was learned in elementary school back then. And whenever the children's hair got longer, they had to put a piece of paper on the table in front of them and comb their hair out. Hordes of lice came to light.

There is another particularly nice anecdote. On the outskirts of Rautenberg, there was a house where an ancient woman had lived for ages. The wandering boys kept seeing this old woman walking into the forest, and the boys were sure that she was definitely a witch who was looking for herbs in the forest to practice black magic. One day at school, when the teenagers were talking about the witch again, their teacher "Graybeard" sat down with them. "I'll tell you a story about the old woman," he said, peering at the boys over his round glasses. Everyone drew closer together in excitement and listened, because "Graybeard" was good at telling stories. The old woman had been the most beautiful girl in the whole village a long time ago, that's how he began the story. And all the young men fell in love with her, even those from the "blue bloods." But the young woman chose one from the village. He was the most beautiful and strongest of all. So they built a house outskirts of the village and made the land around it cultivable. They painted the house in bright colors and everywhere beautiful and fragrant flowers were planted. They swore eternal love for each other, but then the man had to go to war against the French in 1870.[15] When they said goodbye, he said that he would come back soon and she promised to wait for him as long as possible. But when the war was over, he didn't come back. And since then she has been waiting every day for him to come home. And every night a lantern burns at the window so that he can find his way to her. After William heard the story and he walked past her house again while wandering around at night and saw the lantern, it touched him very much and he wished that her husband would return home soon. Since then, no one has called the old woman "witch" anymore.

Then mother Ida fell ill with bovine tuberculosis. A disease that can spread from an infected cow to humans if they drink their milk. The petite mother quickly deteriorated physically. But she didn't let it show, as much as she could, she continued to bravely take care of the house and children. But in the spring of 1929 there was no more hope. She was spitting blood and suffering terribly. She died a few hours before sunrise. The priest present spoke of salvation. William, who was only 14 years old, ran out of the house crying and into the forest. He went in deeper and deeper. He sat in a small clearing and mourned, praying to God. From an early age he felt the power of nature, "Mother Nature," as he called her, and her beauty, which gave him new courage. William was a believer in God all his life. And he had a clear vision of God and how he would communicate with him. He didn't fold his hands or look down. God, William said, would want to see children created in his image as equals. Not on the floor. William remained skeptical of the institution of the church well into his old age. He rejected condescension. Not only by clergy, but in life in general, he didn't like being ruled over. He wanted to be free. And he also communicated this in his later TV career. William's mother wanted her sons to learn a trade. So after their death they all started teaching. One became a butcher, the other made cheese. William learned the trade of saddler and upholsterer in the village. He was hired and trained by Mr. Tomescheit, who worked a lot for the "blue bloods." Mr. Tomescheit had a two-story house in town. The shop was downstairs and he lived upstairs with his wife. The apprentices also lived there and worked six days a week. Only Sunday was free, and on that day the boys always played football. Oh, William loved football. One day a painter traveling through the country came to Rautenburg. He went from one estate to the next and painted the lords' houses, or a portrait, or even landscapes. The children called the artist "frogman," because of what he looked like a frog and also spoke so broadly out of the corner of his mouth. Whenever William could, he watched the frogman. He could paint a landscape in a hurry. This man impressed him, and William also wanted to paint. Like the frogman. Decades later he still remembered the itinerant painter who had so impressed him. After William had been an apprentice for two years, his dream of painting came a little closer. Mr. Tomescheit, his teacher, also looked after the nobles' carriages. He upholstered them, provided them with leather harnesses, and also painted the carriages with beautiful decorations. Since William was clever, he was allowed to do this work from then on and decorated the carriages with painted roses and intertwined leaf tendrils. His teacher was satisfied and William felt like an artist for the first time. Feel good! One of his school friends was Heinz Höller. His father was one of the wealthy landowners in the area. And when he wanted to have a wall in his house painted, Heinz made sure that his friend William got the job. William was thrilled when he saw the large blank wall surrounded by heavy dark wood paneling. He mixed color pigments and oil together and thought about what the squire would like. He actually wanted to paint a horse. Galloping and with flowing mane. But he knew the popular motifs of those days and painted a hunting scene with a deer and a lion, a dense forest and mountains. All in all, a beautiful picture, the landowner was thrilled, and from then on William was allowed to paint in many manor houses. Many years later he visited his friend Heinz in his father's house. The mural was still there, but the colors were all faded or chipped. The colors he mixed did not have the right proportions and, as William reported, in many manor houses they simply painted over his works white.

When the global economic crisis[16] came and more and more people lost their jobs, it was also felt in East Prussia. William had completed his education, but Mr. Tomescheit could not and did not want to employ him any further. A source of income was needed. Since he could play the fiddle very well, he joined forces with some of his friends. Heinz was also there. The five of them then founded a "Hungarian gypsy band," as it was called in those distant days. So they traveled all over East Prussia and visited all the towns. In summer they slept under the open sky, in winter they also played for shelter and something to eat. They wore colorful vests and shirts when they played music, and they played everywhere. At weddings, village festivals and inns, they took advantage of every opportunity. Although they usually only received a little money, they received even more beer for their performances. As he later said, it was a beautiful time and, above all, characterized by freedom.

As a frontline soldier in the Second World War

Around 1935 he met his future wife Margaret. She came from one of the neighboring villages, and after they married, their daughter Heidi was born two years later. Margaret was a beautiful and warm-hearted woman, with dark curly hair and a warm smile. But the young family's happiness didn't last long, because when the Second World War broke out, William also had to join the military. At some point before the war, his father died in an accident at work when he was run over by a train. William blamed the Nazis for this, but no further details are known. In 1940 William Alexander joined the „Landesschützen-Ersatz-Bataillon 1" in Tilsit (his dog tag number was 1 E.I.R23 NA # 11). He served in the Wehrmacht with the rank of sergeant. This is what it says in the German edition. However, after the biography was published, I received documents from his time in the Wehrmacht from a German authority (Federal Archives Department of Personal Information on the First and Second World Wars). This shows that, according to his own statements in his autobiography, he served as a senior sergeant (Oberfeldwebel). Unfortunately, there are few anecdotes from that dark time, but they paint a clear picture of him. He hated war and he loved humanity. William liked to call himself a lousy soldier and said that his superiors probably didn't like him much. Nevertheless, he must have taken his duties seriously; he was wounded a total of four times. When he was once responsible for ensuring that all the soldiers were present during a train transport to the front, the following story happened. The train had a long stop at a station and some soldiers came to him and said that their parents or loved ones lived in the neighboring town, not far away. And they asked if they could stop by for a moment. William knew that this was of course strictly forbidden. This could be seen as desertion, and so he warned the soldiers to come back in time and not to get caught, otherwise they would all be put against the wall. William had compassion for the soldiers, and from then on, whenever the train had to wait longer at a station, soldiers always came with the same wish, and each time he admonished them and then looked away so that they could visit their loved ones. They all always came back. Once, however, an officer caught him "looking away" and barked at him: "Corporal Alexander, you should be shot!" He froze, but then the officer just shook his head slightly, he probably also felt pity for the soldiers, and turned around turned around and left again. During the course of the war he was then transferred to Norway. There they were taken from one small island to the next and had to dig trenches, tunnels and the like. A small boat would regularly come from the mainland loaded with a few officers and they would then check the soldiers' work.

One day, William came up with the clever idea of setting up a post that would immediately warn his comrades with a red flag as soon as the boat is coming. Because, why should they dig when there were no officers on the island? However, something went wrong and the boat landed before the comrade had given the signal. At the very last second, the guard waved the flag and everyone suddenly jumped into the trenches with their shovels, but the arriving officer immediately saw through the game and had William transferred to the Russian front in a rage. Not much is known about the terrible time there; in his memoirs he only wrote that they were in trenches opposite each other with the Russians and that sometimes one side attacked, sometimes the other. One day his trench was overrun and he was knocked unconscious by a Russian with the butt of his rifle. But one memory is very moving. During a so-called rest period, which was taken whenever possible so that a unit of troops could recover and regenerate, he walked through a forest. Somewhere in the middle of Russia. And he came to a small river with an old wooden bridge, which he also crossed. Fish could be seen in the river. Suddenly a Russian man appeared at the other end, tall and powerfully built. Both soldiers had a rifle, but neither made any move to use it. So William slowly walked up to him, smiled and spoke to him in German. He said something to the Russian. That he would now like to go fishing or something like that. The Russian also smiled at him and came towards him, saying something in Russian. Even if neither understood the other, they hugged each other and smiled, then both turned around and disappeared into the forest. Although William was afraid that he would get a bullet in the back, nothing of the sort happened.

Shortly before the end of the war, William was wounded for the fourth time, a bullet hit him again, and he was taken to a hospital near the Rhine. The Americans were already on the other side of the river Rhein, and no one had any serious doubt that the war would soon be lost. Even William, who had been in the hospital for several weeks, had little desire to lose his life so shortly before the end of the war. Once a week, trucks came to the hospital and brought the recovered soldiers back to the front. One week to the west against the Americans, the next week to the front against the Russians. When the trucks arrived again and collected the soldiers, this time they were going west again, William had an idea. He knew he would be released the next week and taken straight to the Eastern Front. But if he was going to be taken prisoner, he thought, then it would be better not to be with the Russians. William wanted to be captured by the Americans instead. So he went to the senior doctor on duty and told him that his unit was currently fighting against the Americans in the west, and since the trucks in front of the hospital were going exactly there, he asked if he could go with them. He's almost recovered. The senior doctor, an older man with alert eyes, quick comprehension and a good-natured nature, immediately understood what was going on and let him go with a wink. When we arrived at the front, or what should have been a front, much of the former strength was no longer there for a long time, so the question arose as to how best to surrender. William was taken to a town near Strasbourg called Niedernai. The Wehrmacht faced General Patton's army[17] and William commanded a small squad of eight men. Of course, he used to command ten times his troop strength, but now there was no more. And his men were rather pitiful too. Old men and half children. But each of them was equipped with a bazooka to stop the American tanks. William swallowed internally. How could you surrender when you were on the front line with bazookas? So he and his men lay under cover along a path until one morning the American tanks suddenly burst out of the forest with a loud roar. Followed by infantry, they came straight toward William's position, and he felt that his last hour had come. But luckily his men didn't even think about wanting to die a hero's death. As the tanks approached, they all dropped their bazookas and suddenly disappeared in all directions. William was happy about it and also withdrew and found a place to spend the night in the village. The next morning the town was occupied by American soldiers, and a captured group of Germans sat on the street with their hands raised. So he also surrendered and was very happy that the war was now over for him. This happened on November 27, 1944. The prisoners were loaded into freight wagons that already contained all sorts of boxes. William and his comrades sat on these boxes, which was much more comfortable than sitting on the ground. They didn't know where they were being taken, but the train was heading south. Regularly, whenever the train stopped, the American soldiers opened the carriages and gave the prisoners something to drink. But they received no food, and the men's stomachs began to growl. Was that harassment? William noticed that every time the Americans opened the wagon and saw the men sitting on the boxes, the soldiers looked at each other in surprise and shook their heads. They also always made a few comments about the "krauts" and laughed. After many more breaks in the journey without food, William and the others eventually knew why they were not receiving food. One of his comrades took a closer look at the boxes they were sitting on. They contained all the food rations for the Germans. They laughed heartily at themselves and at that day they had a really good time. The train stopped in Marseille and from there they were taken to the prison camp 401.[18] A large area, fenced in, guarded and provided with barbed wire. There wasn't much else there. Every day an American officer came to the camp in a jeep to select some Germans for work. Sometimes they were looking for someone who could speak English, sometimes a baker or an electrician. Everyone wanted out of this camp, including William. And every day when the officer came back, he hoped that an artist would be sought today. But an artist was never sought. So William decided he would report the next day. No matter what kind of job they were looking for, he would get in touch. The following day a hairdresser was needed and William answered. The officer immediately took him with him and drove him to a camp. There were barracks and beds, everything was neat and clean, and he was led to a building. Downstairs there was a bar, an officers' club, upstairs there was a room with a hairdresser's chair and all the equipment a hairdresser needed for his work. Now things got serious. William had no idea how to cut hair. But luckily he got into conversation with a prisoner who also worked as a hairdresser. He gave him tips on how to cut, how to put the paper around the neck, and what to pay attention to. That would get him by. The next morning the first customer arrived, a captain in the US Army. William's pulse skyrocketed and his fingers trembled. He was so excited that he even forgot to put the strip of paper around his neck. A large part of the hair that had been cut slipped under the captain's shirt, who had to scratch himself repeatedly. Also, the haircut he got cut looked absolutely terrible. That wasn't a hairstyle, it was an insult to the profession of every hairdresser. But the captain, no doubt sensing the nervousness and fear, just thanked him politely and left. William later wrote that if he had cut a German officer's hair like that, he would certainly have been imprisoned. But William developed ambition. If he was going to do this work, then he wanted to do it well. And he kept getting better. Yes, he got really good, and while cutting he joked with the soldiers, who really liked his style. They called him "Bill," and he kept that nickname throughout his life. William was good with people. He always had an open nature and approached people, which earned him a lot of sympathy and friendship. In the officers' club under his hairdresser's room there were always almost empty bottles lying around, and William, who became friends with the manager, was allowed to take them with him. From then on, while he was editing, he also offered the soldiers a drink in addition to making small talk in broken English. The soldiers really took him to their hearts, and when they came to get his hair cut, they brought him small presents. Downstairs in the officers' club there was a box with paints and brushes in the corner that one of the soldiers had left lying there. Since no one wanted her back, William was allowed to keep her. As a thank you, he painted a beautiful young lady on one of the walls, scantily clad in a bikini. The soldiers were thrilled. William also asked the officer in charge if he could decorate his hairdressing room with pictures he painted himself. The officer liked the idea and even arranged for William to get canvases and more paint. It didn't take long before one of the soldiers asked him while he was cutting his hair if William could paint him a painting of his family and handed him a photograph. He would then send the picture to the USA as a Christmas present. And so it happened that the prisoner of war and hairdresser William, whom the soldiers affectionately called "Bill," was still able to work as an artist. Then the war was over and the prisoners were gradually released. One day Captain Spatz approached William and a long-lasting friendship developed between them, far beyond the war. Captain Spatz also expressed the wish that he could get a picture, which William was happy to do. Spatz was thrilled by the picture and patted William on the shoulder: "Come with me, I have something to show you, Bill." The captain led him into a room with windows and beautiful daylight. "Here, Bill, I wanted to show you this. This is your new studio. You're in much better hands here." William couldn't believe his eyes. Paints, brushes, canvases, good light for working. He could hardly believe it. And he would soon have plenty to do. Always more US soldiers wanted a picture, and William painted tirelessly, working out every detail. Which, by the way, wasn't that easy, because the more awards there were on the uniform, the more precisely he had to represent them. The soldiers patted him on the shoulder appreciatively and said that Bill would become a rich artist in America. In these days the seed was planted in his head, which would germinate and gradually ripen. America! What an exciting idea. William had to report to Captain Spatz several times. William should have been allowed to leave the camp long ago; he was free long ago. He was officially a prisoner of war from November 28, 1944 to June 4, 1946. But he stayed. He stayed and continued to paint tirelessly. Because where should he go? His homeland of East Prussia was occupied by the Soviets, and he didn't know where his wife Margaret and daughter Heidi were either. Were they even still alive? Nothing pulled him away from this place. How long he actually stayed in the camp is not known. But after he had to report to the captain again, he literally threw him out. "Bill, there are only a few officers left in the camp, and you. The camp is being dissolved, you have to leave now." He handed William all the necessary papers. However, he just looked down sadly. "Do you really have no place to go?" Captain Spatz put his hand on William's shoulder and gave him another piece of paper with an adress on it. "Here, Bill. If you don't know where you want to go, then go to Giessen.[19] A friend of mine opened a bar there and he will help you (He received around $20 a month for his work as a prisoner of war. When he was released from captivity, he was paid $282.20).

So William then drove to Giessen. It was a chaotic, a bad time. Almost everything was destroyed. Families were separated and those returning from the war did not know where their relatives were or whether they were even still alive. And everyone had to see how they could survive. Captain Spatz's friend ran a bar there for the US soldiers called "The Cup and Saucer." There was the opportunity to have fun there, there was alcohol and music, and undoubtedly nice ladies who were very happy with her had their own business model. William was able to find accommodation there and he was able to work as an artist again. He painted posters and advertising flyers for the bar. That's how he got by in those days. At night he often went to the river, where he fished, where William dreamed of a better life. Suddenly he heard a noise, a man approaching him. William immediately hid because it was an uncertain time. The man did the same, apparently not noticing William in the dark. So both of them peeked out of their hiding place curiously, and since there was probably no danger, they greeted each other. The man also came from East Prussia, and so the two quickly became friends. From then on they met regularly to fish or talk. One day his new friend William let in a secret: "You know, a while ago I saw some people from the black market burying their goods at night. When they left, I branched out and built my own bunker. We're friends and I'll show you where he is. You are welcome to take what you need." A few days later William saw him for the last time. After that he was gone, just gone. People came and went in those days. He also reported another contact. In Giessen he met an old comrade who had lost an arm in the war. To make ends meet, he kept himself afloat by stealing wallets. He tried his luck with drunken US soldiers who were on their way to the amusement ladies. One day, when William met him again, "Onearm," he later no longer remembered his name, was beaten black and blue. A group of soldiers caught him pilfering and punished him thoroughly. One day "Einarm" also disappeared from the face of the earth. People came and went. William stayed in Giessen and a few years passed before he received news that his wife and daughter were still alive. They were still in the Soviet occupation zone, from which he then brought them to Giessen. William later wrote that the worst things happened to his wife there. He didn't say what, but it's not that hard to guess. Finally, in Giessen in the early 1950s, they were all together again and life improved. William, thanks to his contacts with the Americans, got a job as a printer in the US Army quartermaster's office in Giessen, and the family moved into a small apartment. But there was still his dream of being an artist. America. Why not to America? This thought drove him crazy. His superior was a colonel who was very fond of William. Immigrating to America wasn't easy, so the Colonel advised him to try Canada instead. Canada was large and sparsely populated, so he would have a good chance there. The colonel also took care of all the immigration papers. The wish became a decision and he discussed it with Margaret. He would move to Canada and bring the family with him as soon as he could afford it. They celebrated Christmas 1951 together in Giessen, after which his big adventure would begin.

Across the pond

After saying goodbye to Margaret and Heidi with a heavy heart, William, now 37, drove to Bremerhaven to embark for Canada. In addition to a few belongings, he also took a small toolbox with him. He wanted to build a wooden house for his family and himself in the sparsely populated country, and it would certainly be difficult to get tools there. So he packed a hammer, a slightly bent saw and various rusty nails and happily carried the toolbox with him. A wonderful house could be built with this. t would be a nice house and they would build a farm and have cows. After a journey that lasted around two weeks, he finally landed in the port city of Halifax,[20] in the province of Nova Scotia.[21] He reported to the immigration authorities directly at the port and presented his papers. The officer checked the documents, took a closer look at the immigrant's luggage and then wanted to know what he had in his little toolbox. William proudly showed him the hammer, saw and nails. The officer just frowned in disbelief and looked at the German with wide eyes. Did this German really think there were no tools in Canada? Laughing, he stamped William's papers. Now the great adventure could finally begin. But first he went to the dock again and took his toolbox out of his luggage. He threw the box with the rusty nails and the lousy tools in a high arc into the harbor basin, and it is probably still there today.

In order to get his bearings, he first spoke to some dock workers, who were happy to give him information and also had some advice for him. First he looked for a room. On Wellington Street, for $50 a month, on the first floor, directly above a shop, he found his first home in his new home. Even if William wanted to work as an artist, he first looked for a job, anything, so that he could pay his not small rent. And William was busy. If he had a goal, he achieved it. He was actually very hardworking, although in later years he also said that he liked to be lazy. From then on he worked in a printing shop for 60 cents an hour. At night, for the same rate, he was cleaning in a hotel. And in the meantime he painted his pictures. He was allowed to display some of them in the shop below his room, and he often sold one there. William's portrait paintings, which had already impressed US soldiers, increasingly found sales in Halifax. The rest of his life changed on the day where Audrey O'Brien came to see him. She had seen one of William's portraits in the shop below his room and wanted to take painting lessons from him. She was an elegant and resolute young lady with curly blonde hair who came from a wealthy family. Since her fiance was still studying medicine and they both wanted to get married, she wanted to use the time to learn painting. William's English was still quite imperfect at the time and he never lost his

German accent, so he offered Audrey the chance to look over his shoulder. His first student. A friendship developed between the two of them, and little by little Audrey learned more about his life. One day he told her that he would have to save for five more years before he could bring his family from Germany to Canada. When the painting lesson was over, Audrey said she would pick him up in the car tomorrow to show him something. William was curious, but he didn't think anything special of it. When she picked him up the next day, they went straight to immigration. She resolutely addressed the officer: "We are here to bring Mr. Alexander's family to Canada." She put $600 on the table. William didn't know what to say. He had never seen such a chunk of money in one pile before. How should he get this amount just pay back? It should be noted that Audrey never claimed that amount. When Margaret and Heidi arrived in Halifax weeks later, William and Audrey were standing at the pier. Audrey brought a bouquet of flowers. William had never seen a larger bouquet of flowers before. Audrey also opened various doors for William through her good contacts. His portraits were increasingly sought after, and so more and more of him were painted. He also got some new students from Audrey's environment.

He never missed a chance to earn something. Of course, everything didn't always go well. When he was offered the opportunity to work a few shifts in the bakery, William performed so well and so hard that the owner immediately wanted to train him to be a baker. But this was not well received by the other apprentices, all strong boys from Halifax. It wasn't possible that a „kraut" from Germany could overtake them. And before the boys would explain it to him clearly with their fists, he basically dismissed himself and resigned immediately. After he portrayed an older man who was very satisfied with his work, he offered him the opportunity to earn some extra money. The older gentleman was a big shot at the railway, and around Christmas time the railway was always looking for hardworking hands. William immediately accepted and traveled through Canada as a dishwasher on the train. He passed through many large cities, and when the train had a longer stop there, he always looked around eagerly. Once he discovered a printing shop, and William just walked in. Let's see if he could get a job here with his skills. Not that William seriously wanted to change his job that day. But, you can take a look at what your own market value is like. The boss welcomed him warmly, and William immediately listed what he could do as a printer. In Halifax he was still paid 60 cents an hour in the printing shop. Here, in a bigger city, he was playing poker and said he could start for 80 cents an hour. His counterpart just laughed: "Mr. Alexander, if you can really do all that, then I'll even pay you three dollars an hour." William thanked him to consider it. He was amazed at what he was supposed to get. In the next town, which was already a real big city, he repeated his experiment. He would get four dollars an hour. At the end of the trip, in Toronto,[22] someone even offered him five dollars. Back at Margaret's, to whom he excitedly reported everything, he made another decision: „Margaret, let's go to Toronto." And Margaret, who loved her husband more than anything and who always supported her husband, agreed . But one may doubt whether she happily agreed. Another move was coming, and it wouldn't be the last. The really big adventure was just beginning very slowly.

We need to talk about it for a moment: "Happy bucks" and "lousy bucks"

For most of his life, William was not wealthy, and he made do with it. He didn't have an obsessive need to be rich. He also knew little about the nature of money, except perhaps that he knew it was good to have it. But he was never a businessman, as we will find out later. If he had money, he spent it freely. He used it like an artist would use it. He had ideas and expressed himself with those ideas. He implemented all kinds of projects, many of which failed miserably, but he always took it with humor. And if he didn't have any money, that was fine with him. Coming from a poor background, he was able to be modest. This was the case in East Prussia, and later also in Canada and the USA. When he drove through the country with his partner, they slept in the car or in the open air if necessary. The financial breakthrough came late, in 1974, when he was already 59 when his TV show "The Magic of Oil Painting" flickered on the television. "Happy bucks" and "lousy bucks," William used these two terms often. He mused about it in almost every episode of his TV show. And there was a worldview behind it. His worldview. Lousy money was money earned dishonestly. By cheating someone, for example - or by fighting wars to make money. There is a nice anecdote about this: He experienced it himself once when he had just emigrated to Canada. He wanted to sell his small car and buy a VW bus instead. So he went to a car dealer and William was completely impressed. This salesman, with his warm smile and charming manner, was terrific. And he made such a lucrative offer to William that he just had to take it. An almost new VW bus, barely used and in great shape. He believed everything about this salesman. And so they made a deal, and when the car dealer said, "Mr. Alexander, don't you want to read the contract?" He just waved it off: „We've discussed everything, why should I read it?" William later remembered that he would have blindly bought everything from this man. However, after he set off in the VW bus, it stopped after a few kilometers. In a workshop it turned out that this car was neither new nor in top condition. William went back to the car dealer in a rage. However, the friendly salesperson with the warm smile was suddenly no longer there and another employee came instead. William was beside himself: "How could he sell me such an old car?" Unimpressed and almost emotionless, the colleague simply said, not even looking at the contract: "But, Mr. Alexander. "Haven't you read the contract?" It clearly stated there that the car was old and not in good condition. William understood that the dealer's whole manner was just a show to lull him into signing the contract without reading it. But he didn't want to give up so easily and went to open legal advice. After waiting for a few hours, he explained the situation to a lawyer. He just looked at the contract briefly and asked if he couldn't read it. William was annoyed about this for a long time, probably most of all at himself. For him, this shabby way of earning his money was "lousy bucks."

But even if you are honest about your wages and bread and butter, there are "lousy bucks." Namely, whenever you do a job just to somehow make ends meet. He said that if in your professional life you are only looking forward to having two weeks of vacation once a year, and otherwise you only do something so that you can pay the rent and you don't feel like doing what you do, you If you have to force yourself to go to work in the morning, then that's not a good life. Then you make lousy money and don't understand life. "Happy bucks," the good money, the happy money, is what you always earn when you do an activity that brings you fun and gives you joy. No matter what kind of activity it is. If it fills you up, if it makes you happy, then it's good money. Even if it may be little that you earn, the time, your own positively filled life, that is what is important. You hardly know it. Was he a painting philosopher or a philosophizing painter?

The long road to becoming a "Happy Painter"

The family felt comfortable in Toronto, even though in the 1950s the city was far from what it is today. Wife Margaret worked as a furrier, William in the printing shop. He also painted and even took lessons at an art school. His boss, a very wealthy man who was fond of horses and owned at least two dozen racehorses to support him, held the German in high esteem. William was hardworking and he learned. And very quickly. William was also familiar with all the old printing presses. things that no one else could wait for. And when you gave him an assignment, William just said to give him a week, or sometimes two. And then he implemented what was desired in the best possible quality. One day his boss made a million-dollar deal with the government. His company was supposed to capture medical X-ray images on microfilm. A technology that was still quite new at the time and was far from being fully developed. Of course he turned to William to make it happen somehow. And William knelt down and tinkered around, because the difficulty was that the x-ray image was usually unclear and important details were missing. So he experimented tirelessly with the lighting, this or that. In short, in the end he succeeded. His boss was enthusiastic and then offered him a new, even better paid position. But William hesitated. What had happened to his dream? He wanted to be an artist. And now he was a printer. Although he earned money to support himself, that wasn't his dream that he lived here. He wanted to live the life of an artist. Free and self-determined. So he decided to give up his permanent position. Much to the dismay of his wife Margaret.

After William became publicly known as a painter in America, he repeatedly addressed this topic in his TV show (The Magic of Oil Painting). Before he started painting, he always gave a passionate short speech. He often implored people to always ask themselves what they wanted to do with their lives. And he said they would lead happy lives if they did what was important to them. You shouldn't work for 14 days of vacation a year just to exist. They should live their lives actively and do what they want and what is important to them. That way they would be free and they could lead a happy life. You just have to dare and want it. William remained true to himself and his motto throughout his life, as we will find out dramatically elsewhere.

William painted a lot. Portraits, but also the landscapes he loved that depicted mother nature. He particularly hit the nerve of his time with his landscapes; landscape scenes hung in almost every apartment at the time. He also had a small gallerist who sold his pictures. 30 percent for William, the rest for the partner. Things went well for a while, but then the relationship ended. And once again chance came to his aid. He met the owner of a hardware store. He was so impressed with the pictures that he hired William directly to paint in front of the customers. He set up his easel between the shelves and created portraits. And it worked. One day a lady came up to William and said, "Mr. Alexander, you deserve a better place to paint." The lady, a Mrs. Parker, quickly recognized his potential. Her husband was a big shot at the venerable Hudson's Bay Company store,[23] and she literally pulled William out of the hardware store. From then on he painted under significantly better conditions. First, William was taken to a store window with his easel and people stood in the street and watched in fascination. Later it was used in the market. Sometimes in the outerwear department, sometimes in the china department. Always where the company management wanted to attract customers. The concept worked and during these years he was hired by many shopping centers. Toronto, Vancouver,[24] Montreal[25] and down to the USA. The shopping centers became his studio. William had a VW bus with which he toured from center to center. He also had a license that allowed him to sell his paintings on the street from his car. This bus was a real eye-catcher. It was light blue, and William painted the whole bus with colorful fish and plants. The bus looked like a moving aquarium, with all sorts of colorful fish depicted on the windows. Up on the roof there was a rack for the easels, and on the doors was the slogan: "The Old Master Painter from the Faraway Hills." He loved that time. He painted his pictures in front of an audience and joked with them, making a real show of them. He flirted with the young women as well as their mothers. The audience loved him and the show he put on while he painted his pictures. Many of the spectators followed him from center to center to experience him, and he was announced on posters: "The master painter WB Alexander - the artist from behind the mountains - will be with us in the shopping center from 9 a.m. to 5 p.m. on Monday. "He was praised in this and similar ways. To make him seem a little more important, it was also read that he would soon be starting a big tour from Canada to the USA to South America. People came and they also bought. However, William recognized a problem. Painting his pictures took time, and the oil paint still had to dry. It often took three weeks for a painting to be finished, all in all. Although he regularly sold his pictures, but by the end of the month he couldn't produce enough pictures to earn enough. He was aware that he wouldn't get off to a good start, there wasn't enough either way. His wife Margaret already advised him to go back to work in the print shop. William looked for a solution. At first he painted smaller paintings, of which he was then of course able to produce more. But unfortunately he could only sell them for less money. He thought for a long time, then a brilliant idea came to him. He would change his entire painting technique. It was in the early 1960s when he developed his "wet-on-wet technique," but more about that in the later chapter. This style of painting enabled him to paint complex paintings - landscapes, still lifes, floral motifs, whatever - in just 30 minutes. That was a revolution, it gave him completely new opportunities. He painted large canvases. The formats were the best to sell, and he used large, wide brushes, like those from the hardware store, to paint. This was considerably quicker than with the small artist's brushes. He also disposed of the commercially available small painting spatulas. William took a hardware store putty and sanded it into the shape he wanted. His "almighty" painting knife was born.

Now he could produce enough. When he painted and the audience surrounded him, he created his works in a very short time. However, one day, while painting in a shopping center, this is what happened. He was currently creating a virtuoso still life. The motif was a violin on a violin case. After about half an hour the work was created. And it was good, very good. A man had been watching the entire time. He was a musician and he was fascinated by this picture. He wanted to buy it. William told him the price, $160. That was a lot of money. The musician replied that he couldn't pay that much for the picture, a maximum of $60. They negotiated for a long period of time, went for coffee together and continued negotiating. The musician said he couldn't spend that much money on a picture that was created in 30 minutes. William replied that it took him years to learn to paint like that, and even a doctor who removes an appendix in a few minutes gets paid a four-figure amount for it. The musician generally agreed with him, but, he said, since he saw how quickly it was done, his inner voice told him that he couldn't spend that much money on it. Of course, if he hadn't seen how the work was created, he would have paid $300. So the musician didn't end up buying it, but he did give him some advice. "Bill," he said, looking deeply and seriously into his eyes. "I'll give you some good advice. Paint these wonderful pictures. But never show people how to do it." Around this time, her marriage to Margaret was falling apart. They had experienced many ups and downs since the end of the war. The grueling life of an artist, with all the low blows, the endless back and forth, eventually became too much for her. And now, there daughter Heidi married a dashing young man and left the house when they separated. Contact quickly faded, including with his daughter. William lived as before: he painted in shopping centers, he sold paintings and gave private lessons. He also had an agent who sold his paintings for him. At the time he was living modestly outside Montreal. At the end of 1962 he had his first exhibition of his own. It took place in Toronto, in the legendary Casa Loma.[26] He sold well and made other important contacts.

He was always good with people and was a charmer. William could make anyone feel special. He now gave more and more lessons, especially in higher class circles, and he still toured the galleries. But the big breakthrough was still a long time coming.

The idea came to him to try his luck in California. He packed all of his paintings and easels into his "moving aquarium." It would be laughable if he didn't find galleries in Los Angeles that wanted to sell his beautiful landscapes. In short, he couldn't find her in Los Angeles. But he made an important contact there. In one of the many galleries where he was unsuccessfully presented, a group of women were repainting a picture. William joined them and looked at the canvases. One of the ladies was Martha Dixon. She was cultured and elegant, interested in many things. She once studied singing in Paris, lived with her husband in a chic villa in the Hollywood Hills[27] and belonged to what is probably called "upscale circles". Smiling, she turned to William and they both started talking. Mrs. Dixon had been taking painting lessons for a long time. Her teacher taught the students to break a picture into countless small dots and paint it piece by piece. She had been working on her painting for months. William shook slightly at the sound Mrs. Dixon had been taking painting lessons for a long time. Her teacher taught the students to break a picture into countless small dots and paint it piece by piece. She had been working on her painting for months. William trembled slightly when he heard her words. You sit there for an eternity looking at a picture. He showed Mrs. Dixon his pictures, which were so different. Mrs. Dixon was thrilled and invited William to her home to give her lessons in his painting technique. William later reported that when he became hungry and his stomach began to rumble, she served him German potato salad with chicken. It was the tastiest potato salad he ever ate. Martha, who was his first student in Los Angeles, became a successful artist in later years. A friendship for life was also formed. But at first he didn't get anywhere as an artist and teacher in Los Angeles. So he first drove back to Canada.

It was around the end of 1962 when, at the age of 47, he decided to set up his own painting school so that he could teach an entire class. William rented a house with four suitable rooms on the outskirts of Toronto for cheap money and from then on taught his painting technique there. He had many students who were eager to learn his style of painting. From the lawyer to the doctor, from the warehouse worker to the housewife. It was almost painted all day long, and he wanted to make "almighty artists" out of everyone. He was still busy. William continued to paint in shopping centers or sell his paintings directly from his VW bus. But he still prospered not. There was enough for bread, but rarely for butter.

At this time, a new woman came into his life: Anna Margarete Nolte (also known as Annegret de Vries). William was selling pictures out of his VW bus when she passed by on the street. Her name was almost like his first wife, but her personality was completely different. She worked in an office in Toronto, was interested in painting, played the gui tarre and wrote lyrics and poems. She was the perfect match for the artist William. She looked after him, she supported him and also had his back - she believed in him wholeheartedly. Both quickly felt that they would belong together until the end of their days. And it would be decades before their relationship began to crack, but in the end all that was left was a deep rift. And William was to blame. He did a lot of things wrong in his life. Not out of malice, he had a warm-hearted and kind character, but he often made wrong decisions in private, which he bitterly regretted afterwards, as his foster son later reported. He always said that he would make these mistakes so that others would learn from them and not imitate them." He regretted the mistake he made with Anna Margarete for the rest of his life, but more about that later. Canadian winters were long and cold. Anna Margarete and William therefore decided, like so many before them, to spend the winter in warm California. He also wanted to make a new attempt to achieve success as an artist in Los Angeles. The VW bus was packed again, this time he would do it smarter. They rented a rental house. It was shabby, but that's why it was so cheap. To find new students to teach, William advertised in the newspaper. The ad was small and it was certainly difficult to find. Still, every day the two of them hoped the phone would ring. But it didn't. „That was a bad plan," William muttered. They would have to do it more cleverly. So William thought about what he had already had success with in Canada. He went to the shopping centers. He was welcomed there with joy, and so he painted in front of an audience again and won students again. His friend Martha Dixon from the Hollywood Hills regularly organized art and cultural events in her villa, to which William and Margarete were also invited. Artists and scholars, wealthy entrepreneurs, politicians and diplomats met there. There was also always the German potato salad that William loved so much. The ladies of this honorable society wore beautiful dresses, the gentlemen wore expensive suits, it was a splendor to see these people. William, who couldn't afford an expensive suit, but was once again lucky. Some time ago he gave painting lessons to the wife of a wealthy entrepreneur in Montreal. Mr. Packer, that was the name of the client, saw William painting in one of the shopping centers and spoke to him. Mr. Packer's wife had partial hand paralysis, but she really wanted to learn to paint. William immediately agreed and gave her the lessons. In his memoirs, William later wrote how lovingly Mr. Packer supported his wife, putting the colors on her palette and cleaning her brushes. This couple touched him deeply. But before I digress too much, let me get to the point. In addition to the payment, William received two gifts. On the one hand, there was a small box containing several malt knives that looked exactly like William's. Mr. Packer had learned that William would sharpen his painting knives himself. "William," said Mr. Packer, "you are a painter and you shouldn't waste your time sanding spatulas." So he quickly had a whole series of painting knives made, all of which bore William's name. He also gave him a suit so that he could move in better circles. And what kind of suit was that. Made for a star. Best materials, elegant shine. William felt like a peacock in it, but it didn't miss its effect. Not even at Martha Dixon's events in the Hollywood Hills. She offered her German friend William the opportunity to exhibit all of his pictures at the next event in her house. It was a success, and in addition to the paintings he sold, he got new painting students. Word of the German's talent got around, and William was able to rent a room for his students. Margarete and he also organized elaborate painting seminars, for which they rented special event rooms in hotels. If a day of teaching at "Happy Painter" cost a student $3, you had to dig deep into your pockets for these seminars, $25 a day, and that was a lot back then and you had to invest that. Margarete took care of the entire organization and William did what he did best. Painting, and presenting his show. But in the end there wasn't much going on. The majority of the income went towards rent, catering service and assistants, and so everything stayed the same. They had their daily bread, but there was still not enough for butter. They did this for a few years. In the winter they were in California, in the spring they went back to Canada and in the winter they came back to Los Angeles in their old VW bus. They had long since moved out of the old apartment building. A gallery owner friend who occasionally sold pictures for William let her live in a room behind his gallery over the winter. This way you could save money. Money that they urgently needed. Because at that time there was a new setback for the two of them. The last time they were in Los Angeles, William had made a deal with another gallery owner. William painted the gallery owner a whole mountain of pictures that he wanted to sell during the year. If William came back in the winter, he would be paid off by the gallery owner. It should have been a hefty sum. But when William drove to the gallery, it was closed. The gallery owner had long since left with all the money, it was rumored, towards the Caribbean. William had enough. Something had to change. He wanted to get away from Los Angeles. Far away.

However, he fell ill that winter; it was probably bronchitis. Since William, like so many freelancers, had no health insurance because it was expensive, he initially tried to cure himself (only when his financial success became apparent did he take out health insurance years later). But that failed and he got worse and worse. Anna Margarete became increasingly worried, and one day she quickly put William in the VW bus full of paintings and drove him straight to the emergency room in Long Beach. A doctor looked at him and then said he needed to be taken to the hospital. For this information he wrote out an invoice for $12 and gave it to Anna Margarete. They then sat in the recording room and waited their turn. They felt uncomfortable. Just being admitted to the hospital would probably cost $500. Where would they get that from? At that moment a young, good-looking doctor came into the room. His name was Dr. Waite and asked loudly who owned the VW bus with all the paintings that was parked across the parking lot down there. Anna Margarete jumped up and shouted loudly: "Here, here he is. And he dies!" Dr. Waite smiled and took them both into an exam room. He grinned and said that you couldn't just let such an artist die. After a thorough examination prescribed Dr. Waite some medication and wrote his bill. Anna Margarete and William watched almost fearfully as the doctor filled out the form. How expensive would that be? When Anna Margarete saw the bill, she was amazed and showed it to William, who also looked to Dr. in disbelief. Waite stared. "That would be $2.75 please!" The doctor laughed and winked at them. He knew this artist couple had no money. William, who was already fearing the worst, thanked him very much and took out the most beautiful painting of all from his VW bus, which he gave to the doctor as a thank you. He was a very nice person, but unfortunately, as William later wrote, he died far too early of a heart attack.

The story of William and his foster son "SandyBandy"

William and his new girlfriend Anna Margarete were both still in their first marriages. Although they lived separately from their respective partners, divorce was out of the question at the time. Especially not if you were Catholic, like Anna Margarete. As the saying goes, the two lived together in a wild marriage throughout their lives. Anna Margarete's husband was a native of Poland who worked as a farmer and was drafted into the Polish army during World War II. He was taken prisoner by the Germans early on, where he did not fare well. After the war, severely traumatized, he emigrated to Canada and met Anna Margarete. They married and lived near Toronto. In 1950 their son Talore was born. But the marriage was difficult and fraught with problems. Her husband regularly had uncontrollable outbursts of anger, called his wife "the devil," and there were regular scenes of violence. It is confirmed that the mother repeatedly had to keep her husband away with a knife in her hand. At some point Anna Margarete couldn't take it anymore and left him and her child too. The little boy was just four years old. From then on he lived with his highly aggressive father. As part of my research for this book, I asked him in the fall of 2023 what his father did for a living. He answered me: "For as long as I can remember, from the first day I started school, he didn't work for a living. But I don't know where he went or what he did. And I was mostly unsupervised the whole time. Even though he owned the house we lived in, it was rented out most of the time." The boy didn't have it easy with his father. One day the school nurse sent him home because he had measles. When we got home, the situation immediately escalated; the father struck him repeatedly and broke the boy's arm. The son reported: "Yes, as a child I was brutally beaten just because I got sick. It was a tenant who took me to the hospital ten days after the break to treat my broken arm." In all those years, the boy only saw his mother twice. The one time his parents tried to reconcile, but it came to an abrupt end. And then again when he was eight years old. He could no longer remember the circumstances. It was spring and his mother came over and brought him a bag of cherries. The son told me in conversation: "I have no idea what we talked about and I don't remember crying or being upset, but I was grateful for the cherries. I had never eaten fresh cherries as I had not yet learned about the neighbors' gardens to plunder before the birds did." Little Talore only found comfort in a cat named "Smokey," and later in a small dog. If his father took out his anger on him again, he would be punished by having to hold heavy objects on his outstretched arm or by brutally pushing his face under the water. And once the little one asked what was wrong with his mother, the father completely freaked out and screamed in his face that his mother was the devil incarnate. Then he struck. Finally one day the authorities intervened, the father was taken to court and the son was initially taken to the home. At the age of 15 he was handed over to foster parents. Here he felt for the first time what a family really was. Despite his ordeal, the boy always did well in school, even above average. Unfortunately, influenced by a bad childhood, the teenager became increasingly inclined to violence. Also unfortunately, at this time he also started taking various drugs.

In 1966, the authorities contacted Anna Margarete and offered her the chance to meet her son. The mother wondered whether she should really meet him. She was overwhelmed when he was little, how could that be now after all these years? William understood her concern and thought for a moment: "You know what, I'm going to Toronto and meet him. I'll take a look at him. Maybe he is nice." Anna Margarete gratefully agreed and an appointment was arranged. William drove his "mobile aquarium" the approximately 600 kilometers from Montreal to Toronto just to meet the boy in a restaurant and see what the boy was like and whether you could even have an intelligent conversation with him . They met in a small bar in the Danforth district[28] and William told the boy that he could order anything he wanted. He did so with shining eyes and there were burgers and fries and William had coffee and cake. He loved all kinds of sweets. William's financial situation was as strained as usual, but he wanted the boy to have a good time that day and not lack for anything. After dinner he gave him some change for the jukebox, and the boy played the Bee Gees up and down. Then they talked. It was a long conversation and the son told him everything we had just learned here. William sensed that the boy wasn't as bad as one might first think. At the end of the visit, he placed his hand on the boy's shoulder and said, „What doesn't kill you makes you stronger." Upon his return, William reported everything to the mother and a meeting was arranged with the boy in Montreal. The authorities took care of all the necessary formalities and would then hand the teenager over to his mother and William in Montreal. For a weekend initially. Decades later the son recalled: Further arrangements were made for me to take the train from Toronto to Montreal where a government official would meet us all for the "handover." On October 7th, 1966 the time had come. It was like a scene from a spy film with a prisoner exchange." William, the mother and the boy arrived late at night in the VW bus because there had been a spectacular car accident, so the road was blocked for a long time. Even the television reported about it. William and Margarete lived in Woodlands at the time, which is about 30 kilometers from Montreal. They rented an old house from 1875 or earlier. Today the place is called Ville de Léry.[29] The houses in this part of the small town were all built on a long street that follows the banks of the St. Lawrence River (or Lac St. Louis, as it was called because of its width at the time was called). Many of these houses were owned by wealthy businessmen and were used as summer homes. William's house was closest to the street. When they arrived everything was dark, but the boy could still see that the old house had a red roof and there was a surrounding wooden veranda that was painted white. It was a simple house with about 80 square meters of floor space on the ground floor. There was a kitchen, a living room, a small alcove and a small bathroom. Most of the walls looked like what is now called "country house style." In the back was William's „studio," a converted pantry that smelled strongly of paint thinner. There were two bedrooms on the upper floor. The furnishings were a bit sparse, and there were oil paintings all over the walls. There were also a noticeable number of easels with finished paintings standing around. All in all, the house was very clean and well-kept, but you first had to come to terms with the constant smell of paint thinner. The boy felt a mixture of curiosity and concern as he entered the house for the first time. He wondered what it would be like to live there, surrounded by all the art and history. He also wondered how he would get along with his mother and William, since he barely knew either of them. He hoped they would be nice and friendly. The next morning there was a sumptuous breakfast. William's famous "European breakfast" or "fish breakfast" for short. He still raves about it today. It consisted of lots of coffee, rye toast, fried eggs and various types of sausage and meat. The highlight of the sumptuous breakfast was always when William prepared his freshly caught fish in a pan. William's breakfast was very popular among his friends because there were always exciting conversations and it could last for hours in a very sociable manner. William and Margarete also regularly offered beer and liquor. They also offered the 16-year-old alcohol while eating. He later jokingly commented: "They offered me beer and liquor with dinner, even on the first day. They were Europeans and believed that learning to be responsible social drinking at home begins at a reasonable age. I think I was of a reasonable age. I never embarrassed myself or her, never." Later that day, the boy watched as William painted a beautiful landscape in half an hour at his home. Around 90 x 60 cm in size. He still remembers the measure today. The boy sensed that William was something very special *(he jokingly told me in November 2023 that William was always very clean and always smelled good. Unless he was painting. Then he smelled strongly of paint thinner and usually had various paint stains on his belly)*.

While the first meeting only lasted a weekend, plans have now been made to enable a one-year stay. Yes, later the boy was even supposed to move in permanently.The 16-year-old felt safe with William. He noticed him, he listened to him and also made him feel special. So they quickly became friends, and from then on the boy called him "Pop" and William jokingly called him "Sandy" or "SandyBandy." The boy quickly grew fond of William, which was perhaps partly due to the fact that after separating from his wife, he lost contact with his daughter. "SandyBandy" later recalled: "...Pop's enthusiastic nature and generosity were impossible to ignore and simply made you want to be with him. He had charisma... He just made people feel good. It can not be said otherwise. And he let me know that I was special. The first person ever." William and "Sandy" quickly got used to each other and both enjoyed it. William's daughter Heidi was now living her own life and was little interested in her father's career, how he developed from a printer and charming, sly traveling artist to a successful teacher and TV artist. There was also little contact with his grandchildren, but he probably coped well with that because he was never really comfortable with small children. He enjoyed the new fatherly role that he was now able to fulfill all the more. He taught him everything he thought was important. How to catch salmon as well as how to properly cover canvases on a stretcher frame, how to drive a motorboat and how to shoot also needed to be learned. For Christmas the boy even received a real Winchester from William. And his foster son was always amazed at how strong this fat little man was. His short, sausage-like fingers were as strong as vices, and yet he could still use them to handle the smallest brushes. "You have to be able to fix everything yourself," William always said. And there really wasn't anything he couldn't fix himself. Yes, if necessary, he even spontaneously became a "dentist." When his new bridge once pressed against his jaw, he quickly re-ground it in his workshop until it finally fit. He was just very pragmatic. This is also evident in philosophy, which he passed on to the boy. "Good enough is enough!" That was one of the many philosophies in William's life. And it said, in short: "Always apply the right amount of effort for the intended result. Excess is waste." Another favorite saying of his was: "I can make chocolate out of dirt. I made chocolate out of dirt." They often invited friends over. There was always good food, music and a lot of laughter. "Sandy" was regularly "forced to be a bartender" by Bill on these evenings because the boy was very talented at mixing alcoholic drinks. His specialty was the so-called "screwdriver," and you can imagine why it was called that. It consisted of vodka and orange juice. But probably more like vodka and a hint of orange juice.

At some point, Anna Margarete and William made the decision to take the boy in permanently, but the authorities refused to allow them to move in completely because William and Anna Margarete could not yet demonstrate a secure existence at that time. So, for better or worse, the boy had to go back to his foster family. It never happened, not even when William was doing well financially, for the boy to move in with them. But they saw each other often, and the boy changed for the better. William's behavior motivated „Sandy," and he began to believe in himself. He became a good athlete, baseball was his great passion, and with success came self-confidence. The boy completed school successfully, at the top of his class, and he moved out of the foster family immediately after he came of age. At first he made ends meet by doing odd jobs and sometimes sleeping in the open air. William experienced the same thing in his early years in East Prussia. But then he was given the chance to complete a banking apprenticeship, which he completed with flying colors. He became a successful banker. However, a heart attack ended his banking career and he had to take it easy from then on. So he initially decided to become a real estate agent, then later manager of a golf course, but at the end of the day that couldn't really be described as quieter.

Today he lives as a sprightly pensioner with his wife and his aging German Shepherd "Suki" in western Canada. Suki must be an intelligent dog because he vehemently refuses to go outside when it rains and storms. Both have children and a grandchild. In his free time, he works, among other things, on "artificial intelligence" and uses it to create virtual paintings. He also writes a wide variety of articles for an online magazine and is passionately committed to ensuring that his foster father is not forgotten and that he is also recognized for his artistic achievements.

An artists' colony is created

Winter had Montreal firmly in its grip, and the St. Lawrence River[30] froze over more and more in the coastal area. This was exactly the time that all ice fishermen were waiting for. William was also one of those guys who couldn't wait any longer. Of course, he also had one of those portable fishing huts that you pulled directly onto the ice by car. Once the hut was up, you drilled a hole in the ice, sat on a stool next to it and let the fishing line slide down. Of course they recognized it straight away, these fishing huts have no floor but only four walls and a door, and if you had some money, there were also a few modest windows built in. But some of the huts were like an upright shoebox, only made of boards and with a door. Almost all of the boys on the ice knew each other and were like a close-knit community. One of his friends there was an Indian chief whose ancestors had been fishing there for centuries. And no one could do it better than him. At some point, when the ice was thick enough, the heavy bulldozers and snow plows came and created paths on the frozen river. Each path then led to one of these fishing huts. Huge amounts of snow piled up because there were many who were crazy about ice fishing. William's foster son was just visiting and was able to help attach William's fishing hut to the VW bus. "It's going to be a great day," said William happily, wearing a thick jacket and hat as he stowed away his fishing rods. "Sandy" didn't see it as sporty. Fishing wasn't his thing, nor was he seriously into winter. But he came along and tried to act like he was having fun too. So they both sat in silence in the small hut. When he got too cold or too bored, usually the latter, he asked "Pop" if he could take the bus for a bit. William once taught him how to drive the bus, how to change gears and what to watch out for on icy surfaces. That's how William was. He once said that if you can drive on icy surfaces, you can drive anywhere. So William let him have his way and the teenager drove back and forth in the car, accelerating rapidly and then slamming on the brakes and allowing himself to be shaken. William watched from the corner of his eye and then saw his foster son skid and crash into the middle of a snowdrift. Horse and rider, sorry, car and driver were undamaged, apart from a few small dents that both sustained. The boy hoped William hadn't seen it, otherwise he would end up telling him in the future prohibit this fun. When he got back to the hut, he acted as if nothing had happened. William just looked at "Sandy," he looked at him knowingly, the way only adults can look at children and then feel caught. He looked exactly the same and didn't say a word. He smiled at him. Maybe at that moment he was thinking about all the crazy things he himself once did in East Prussia. When the boy turned 18 and visited "Pop" and his mother, they gave him an old Volkswagen from 1957. The fuel gauge was missing and it also had a few dents, but that didn't bother the birthday child. He loved the VW and drove it around Vancouver for hours, even into the mountains, and if it suddenly stopped because the fuel gauge was missing, he always had a small reserve tank with him just to be on the safe side, which William put in him wise foresight.

It was precisely at this time that the idea of starting a new adventure arose. William had a special dream in his head. He wanted to create a place somewhere in untouched nature where artists from all over America and indeed the whole world could come together. He then wanted to teach his students here. Far from the cities. It was in 1968, and he was sure now was the time for that dream. "Fire in!" When, if not now? Their old VW bus, "the moving aquarium," was loaded again. So they drove from Los Angeles northwest, along the coastal road towards Canada. The countless pictures that were squeezed into the bus created a wild mess when you looked into the car. Whenever William and Margarete found a nice viewing spot, they stopped at the side of the road. It happened repeatedly that they provoked a traffic jam, as curious drivers kept stopping to take a look at the bus and the driver. Especially when William set up the easel and painted. Once the police even came and asked William to drive away immediately. At some point along the way they ran out of gas and unfortunately they had run out of money for a long time. A truck driver kindly towed them away and took pity on them both. So he bought a few of his pictures from the VW from William. One for himself, one for his parents, and one for his brother too. William gave him a very reasonable price as a thank you. 25 dollars for a picture. In good days, his gallery owner sold them for ten times as much, of which he only received a small 30% share in the end. So they made it to British Columbia. This Canadian province lies on the Pacific Ocean, just across the US border. William and Margarete knew their way around here. They loved this province, the beautiful, vast nature and the climate. Why shouldn't your dream come true here? They drove back and forth through the province until they found a small spot. Unspoilt and not far from the sea. Near a town called Aldergrove,[31] around 60 kilometers from Vancouver, there that they have their little bit of happiness. The land was around 2.5 hectares in size and not expensive at all. But everything is expensive when you don't have money. But he wanted this piece of land. He wanted to build his wooden house here, his dream would come true here. The next day he went to a bank to take out a $500 loan. That would be enough for everything you need for now. The bank employee looked at the man with the colorful shirt and the strange German accent and said that it wasn't a problem at all and what security he could offer. "Collateral?" William looked at him. "I have no security, but I'm an artist, that's my security." The employee wrinkled his nose and our friend was escorted out. This made William angry. To be treated condescendingly? Not with him.

He thought for a moment, then made a plan. The next morning, Anna Margarete unpacked the "1 million dollar suit" that he received from Mr. Packer. He looked clean, important and significant. So William entered the bank again. He condescendingly dismissed an employee who spoke to him. "I'm just talking to the bank manager." Then he leaned against the bank counter and looked bored. The director, a nice man named McDonald, came out of his office and invited William over. Mr. McDonald wanted to know what he could do for him. "I'm in the area to buy land. Much land. I've just surprisingly found a good piece and we've come to an agreement. But I still need $2,000 as a down payment today. I'll pay you back as quickly as possible." You can't really say who made more of an impression. William or the suit. In any case, he received his check straight away. They bought the property and a lot of wood, cement, tools and nails. They dug a foundation into the night and mixed the concrete. William was in his element, he could create something. Something really wonderful. Here they would live and work, in the middle of nature. At first the wooden house was small and modest, which was what the resources allowed. But every time some money came into the house, they grew. New wood was brought in and William carpentered and hammered tirelessly. More and more rooms were added. And when the work was finished, he made a small pond. It was an idyll, surrounded by cedars and firs. A small path led into the forest and snow-capped mountains rose on the horizon. But for an artists' colony you also needed artists.

And sure enough, they came. Bit by bit. And there were more and more of them. In the end it was an almost family group of twelve art obsessives. At the beginning, only a few fit pensioners from the surrounding area came. They saw William painting in the shopping centers and were looking for something meaningful to do. One of them always jokingly said that he had to avoid a pet dragon at home. In a coffee shop Margarete once met a young woman, her name was Doris. She had just separated from her husband and was completely devastated. Both women quickly started talking and Doris was enthusiastic about this artists' colony. She always wanted to paint. But unfortunately she couldn't afford it financially. Anna Margarete waved her hand and told her not to worry about the pay, but she would fit in so well with the group in Aldergrove. William and Margarete always took people in without charging them anything, that was how they were. By the way, Doris turned out to be extremely talented; she was able to sell her first painting in a diner for a whopping $125. Another exceptional talent was 16-year-old George Rammell.[32] He was a young, flaky drifter who was drawn to the artistic community like a bee to honey. He also had no money and was taken in by William. In return, he always helped when the wooden house was expanded or other work was needed. George was very talented. He enjoyed painting, but was even more fascinated by stones and wood. In Aldergrove he carves beautiful sculptures. Moose,

Bears also a portrait by William that he later installed in his home in Powell River. George Rammel became a famous sculptor and lecturer who is still active in his studio today.

William raved about his time in the artists' colony. During the day everyone worked as usualowned and painted. In the evenings they sat together by the fire and discussed or dreamed about a better tomorrow. At some point Anna Margarete came with her guitar and started playing and singing some of the songs she had written herself. William usually joined in with his fiddle. One of the lyrics she wrote has been preserved; it was one of Williams' favorite songs:

IT´S SPRING AGAIN

It´s Spring again! It´s Spring again!
I feel the breath of May!
Goodbye my love, goodbye my prince,
No longer can I stay.

Last night I heard, a mocking bird
Make fun of me and sing:
„Come out of hid-ding sleepy head,
It´s Spring again! It´s Spring!"

Down yonder at the river bank,
Old Mother Earth is dressed
in purple, yel-low, green and gold,
She wears her Sunday best.

Around the bend, my good old friend,
The restless meadow brook
Sings happy mel-odies for me
There´s Spring in e-ver-y nook.

Up towards the snow-capped mountain peaks,
Above me I must roam,
See eagles soar, on endless skies,
See mighty rivers foam.

From there up high, one last goodbye
The whisp´ring winds will bring:
„Goodbye, my love, goodbye my friend,
It´s Spring again! It´s Spring!"

In the documentary about William already mentioned, there is also a film sequence in which Anna Margarete sings the song and he plays the fiddle for her.[33] Sometimes William also took out his "singing saw". Only a few people know this instrument today. It's basically a large steel saw, like a standard foxtail, but about three feet long. If you bend the saw blade and touch it with the violin bow, you will hear melodic sounds, and if you don't control them, sometimes scary ones. William could play it very well and used it to produce Hawaiian music, to which he then rocked back and forth rhythmically. Anna Margarete also often sang when they were alone while William painted. In her songs she sang about all the adventures they both experienced together. She was an absolute romantic. In the winter months, William and his partner drove back to Los Angeles. As already described, they stayed cheaply. Back in town, there the students from last year quickly gathered again and, as in all previous years, he painted in the large shopping centers and sold directly from his "moving aquarium." Since the artists' colony was not really sustainable and its financial concept had to fail because it was far too open-hearted in accepting people who cost it money but brought in no money, the money for the next summer had to be earned in the winter. They also gradually marketed more and more their color, including the legendary "Magic White," but we'll talk about that in detail shortly. They also now sell brushes and his painting knife, which he originally sharpened himself according to his wishes, to their students. In the 1980s, William wrote that before painting lessons he always asked Anna Margarete whether they currently had more brushes or painting knives in stock. When she said that they currently had more painting knives than brushes, the old fox William decided to work exclusively with the knife in front of the class that day. And if they had more brushes, he decided to conjure up lush forests, bushes and lakes on the canvas with his brushes. They kept their artists' colony alive for four years, but then they decided to sell everything there for cost reasons; a new phase of their life together would now begin. Towards the end of his TV career, at the beginning of the 1990s, he philosophized again in his TV show about how nice it would be if a new artists' colony were founded and sponsors were found for it. Artists from all disciplines from all over North America and indeed the entire world should meet there and exchange ideas. Artists who create something together and strive for a better tomorrow creatively and peacefully. Wouldn't that be wonderful?

The ingenious "Alexander painting technique"

It is long past time that we talked in more detail about his painting technique, with which he was able to "conjure up" such beautiful and complex landscapes, still lifes and even flower arrangements onto the canvas in just 30 minutes. Yes, even more, he even promised that everyone could do the same thing. "In every human being there is an all-powerful creator," as he liked to say on his TV show. And with these words he clenched his fist and laughed into the camera. We already heard that he originally developed this painting technique so that he could produce pictures faster and earn more money. It took William years to perfect this technique, and there were many difficulties that he was slow to perfect, as we will learn. But when he perfected it, he believed he had discovered the Holy Grail and he felt so powerful in front of the screen. Now he was „next to god," as he used to say, and was able to play on the screen of all-powerful creators. The idea of passing this technology on to students came about much later. At some point, William realized that he particularly loved being a teacher and inspiring his students. He wanted to teach the world how to paint because he wanted people to feel good and powerful. He wanted to make the world better. Anyone can create something if they just put their mind to it. He liked to say jokingly: "If you want to paint a happy picture, you have to be happy. If you want to paint a lousy picture, you have to feel lousy." In one of his broadcasts in 1987, William, long a famous TV painter, proudly pointed out once again that this technique he had developed and the „Magic White" were his greatest inventions. He said: "This color and this technique is my life."[34]

In this chapter I will not only discuss his "Alexander painting technique." If you your-self would like to create a painting in this way so that you can follow in the footsteps of our "Happy Painter," you will find valuable tips here that will save you from many failed attempts and frustration. Just try it, you too have an "almighty" artist in you who just wants to get out! Become a creator too. The great innovation in his painting style consists of the combination of three very different components, which William combined perfectly. He had to endure countless experiments and frustrating failures, but then, after many years, everything came together harmoniously and the ingenious "Alexander painting technique" was finally born:

Component 1 - The underground:

In painting, colors are mixed with white to brighten them. This usually happens directly on the artist's palette. William came up with something new because before painting he applied a special white paint to the entire canvas, the so-called - and he developed - „Magic White." Because the canvas was pre-treated and he applied his colors directly to it. A lot of time could be saved. For example, if he took a brush with some red paint and then stroked it over the canvas, it would turn pink. If he applied more red, the color surface became darker. If he continued to distribute the color, it would become brighter and brighter. The "Magic White" he invented is still a bestseller. But the road to market maturity was long. This white also had to have a very special consistency. It had to be liquid, but also not too liquid. He spent nights experimenting again and again with a variety of colors and oils and tweaked their mixing ratios. The right white also had to be found first. There are a lot of different shades of

> W. ALEXANDER'S
> **MAGIC WHITE**
> **No. 1**
> Invented and Successfully Used
> by
> **"The Ole Master Painter from the Far Away Hills"**
> PLEASE STIR WELL BEFORE USING.

Williams paint canister label "Magic White" from 1971[35]

white available in stores (zinc white, titanium white, ivory white, and I don't know what else). In any case, it was not allowed to yellow, and the strength of the pigmentation also had to be right. There have been countless frustrating failures, especially when it comes to choosing the right oil. Only after years did William have a final and satisfactory result, as well as a reliable manufacturer. Please don't pin me down, but I think the mixing ratio for „Magic White" is one part paint and three parts oil. But please only use saffron oil. However, I recommend that you buy it from specialist retailers. This will just save you a lot of unnecessary grief.

Component 2 - The painting utensils:

He also came up with a lot of ideas when it came to painting tools in order to be able to work much faster and still with a lot of detail. His landscapes have countless details. The finest cloud structures, complex reflections and nuanced details in bushes, trees and fields. The whitecaps in the sea are covered in lush detail and in his depictions of mountains you can see every cliff and every snowfield. William loved details, and that's what distinguishes his pictures. An important instrument for these delicate depictions is his "almighty painting knife," which we have already heard about and which he originally cut out of a simple spatula according to his own ideas. Of course, there were already all sorts of different types of painting spatulas, but they were all inadequate for him and his painting technique. He also likes to use large brushes, like the ones you find in hardware stores. 1 inch, 2 inch and 2.5 inch brushes are an integral part of William's painting technique, because a large brush can quickly absorb and release a lot of paint. But would you have thought that such a large, coarse brush could be responsible for the finest details? The brush "loaded" with paint must not have bristles that are too soft. By the way, boar bristle brushes are very suitable. If you then dab them on the canvas, you get countless small areas, dots and lines that simulate a variety of details. In addition to the paint knife and the brushes just mentioned, there is also the fan brush. The name is explained by its shape, and it can also work magic on the canvas (countless new brush shapes have been added over the years, but let's not forget, after all, it's all about selling brushes). These painting utensils, tailored to his needs, allow for an extremely delicate and nuanced style of painting, which looks like a lot of work, even though entire mountain ranges with all their details can be created in just a few strokes, and that can be taken literally. William always said, why make life difficult when there is an easier way. Why spend two days painting a lousy tree when you can create it just as complex with five simple strokes. Besides, William added, it wouldn't be any fun to spend three weeks painting just one picture. He was far too impatient for that.

Component 3 - The oil paint:

Oil painting is usually a very time-consuming painting technique because the paint dries very slowly. That's why it is usually applied in thin layers (glazes). Once this has completely dried, which can take several days, a new layer can then be painted over it. A complete landscape with sky, mountains, trees and water, in which a wealth of reflections can also be seen, takes weeks or months to complete. But William, and he regularly announced this on his TV show with great gestures and temperament, wanted to implement an idea NOW and he also wanted to have the finished picture NOW. Not for three weeks. He didn't have that much patience. He wanted to be spontaneous and create his landscapes, just as it came to him at that moment. But oil painting isn't really suitable for quick and spontaneous work... actually. But William managed to square that circle, you could say. For the fans of nomenclatures, he used a "wet-on-wet painting technique" which he implemented "alla prima." "Wet-on-wet" means that he added more wet oil paint to the wet oil paint. This is nothing generally new, the Dutch masters of the 15th century already worked like this and created fine and soft transitions, usually in the area of clouds and sky or background. "Alla prima" means that he painted the picture in one go. Without dry phases and without major corrections. But the attentive reader will now say, wait a minute, it was just said that you have to let the oil paint dry first before adding a new layer over it. Correct, but - again not. Let me explain it with an example: If you mix red and green paint, which are known to be complementary colors, you get a gray color. So if you, dear reader, apply red oil paint to the canvas and immediately afterwards go over it with green paint, then both colors will smear and mix on the canvas to form a gray tone. But when our friend William first applied red paint and then green paint, surprisingly the two tones didn't smear! This smeant he could paint without drying phases and save a lot of time. But how does the almost impossible work? One would think of magic, and in fact, he used an almost ingenious trick that one has to figure out first. The solution is actually quite simple, and in his painting show, "The Magic of Oil Painting," it looks completely easy. But rest assured, you have to practice, practice a lot, until you succeed satisfactorily. But then you too feel like an "almighty creator" on the screen, to use Williams' words again. The trick is that you use oil paint, each of which must have a certain consistency. If the colors have the wrong consistency, this painting technique won't work, no matter how many times you try.

To begin with, the entire canvas is coated with the liquid "Magic White." If you want to try it yourself, make sure that the white paint is applied very thinly. There should only be a very thin film of color on the screen. But the color film must not be too thin, and that doesn't make it any easier. It takes time to get the hang of it, but eventually it becomes second nature. However, if the color film is applied too thickly, the entire painting technique will no longer work. Now let's talk about the colors you have on the palette. As I said, it's all about the consistency of these colors. What we need is solid oil paint. Very solid and tough oil paint. William always demonstrated by pressing his painting knife onto one of the blobs of paint and then turning the palette over. The knife stayed on the palette. "This is how the color has to be, and nothing else." If you are in the paint store and want to know which oil paint is suitable, then simply open the paint tube. If oil is already dripping towards you, just quickly put this paint back on the shelf. We can't do anything with that. Our paint needs to be tough, so tough that it can barely be squeezed out of the tube. With her our project succeeds. A little tip at this point: If you have paints that are not solid enough, press them onto your palette and then let the paint dry there for a few days.

Now it gets exciting because now we want to paint. So, "Fire In," as he shouted every time he started a picture. There is one basic rule that needs to be followed, regardless of whether you are using a painting knife or a brush. The color that is applied to the "Magic White" must be applied very thinly. William always said jokingly, "We paint with paint without actually applying paint." And indeed, when he applied, for example, ultramarine blue paint for the sky and added a few clouds in a mixture of titanium white and vermilion red, these then With his broad brush he would smudge in circles to create a naturalistic sky, then he would often scrape off the excess paint with his painting knife so that only a very thin layer of paint would remain. Because then we are able to apply color again to (!) this layer. A mountain massif is now painted on the sky with the painting knife. The broad blade of the knife applies the mountain shape in a color mixture of blue and brown, for example, and is wiped downwards with a brush. A spatial depth is already emerging. But now it becomes almost magical. White paint is applied to the "almighty" painting knife and partially poured over the mountain massif. The tough white paint breaks open and with just one stroke, countless small white areas are created that look like countless details. The paint sticks to the bottom layer and thus tears. Now the shadow areas are created. Dull blue paint is applied over the newly created white areas with one stroke of the painting knife. It also tears open and sticks to the bottom layer. The illusion of a complex mountain range was created. Attention, an incredibly important tip at this point: Any color that is applied to a lower layer must be a little more liquid (!!!) than the color underneath. "Liquid" is not to be understood literally. The color is still solid, but a little softer. This can be achieved, for example, by adding a little "Magic White" to the desired color. Anyone who wants to learn this technique has to memorize this sentence, and William repeated it like a mantra: "The thinner paint sticks to the thicker paint!" That's basically the whole secret. "The thinner paint sticks to the thicker paint!" In this way wet paint not painted into each other, but on top of each other! It sounds so simple, but you first have to train it very long and intensively.

Just like with the painting knife, the same goes for the brushes. If, for example, a tree is to be painted, the large bristle brush is dipped in dark green paint. Until it is full and "loaded." William then slammed the brush onto the canvas and with just a few dabs he formed a tree or an entire forest. With a smaller bristle brush, as described, but you can also use almost any hardware store brush as long as the bristles are not too soft, he picked up a lighter tone. Yellowish green to create the sunny side of the tree. Here too, a few dabs on the canvas are enough. The bristles of the brush, as well as the angle of impact, ensure that countless small structures that look like leaves appear on the canvas. Of course, the same applies here: thin application of paint and the top color must be slightly more liquid than the bottom. If you take all of this to heart, then nothing will stand in the way of your artistic career.

The big dreams finally come true

When William was in Los Angeles, he had constantly changing artist agents who were responsible for marketing his works. Sometimes he had people who were not very suitable, but in 1973 he had a young man at his side who was really worth his money. At that time, television was becoming more and more popular and new TV channels were constantly being created. Of course, William didn't miss this either and wondered whether it wouldn't be a great idea if he gave painting lessons on television. For an audience of millions. What a great idea. Then he shook his head and thought, what a lousy idea. Or maybe not? In any case, his artist agent had a similar idea, he wanted to put William on television. There were countless game shows on television, one of which was called „Dialing for Dollars," and the concept was undoubtedly as sophisticated as the concepts of today's game shows. The agent managed to get William on the show with a guest appearance. He would paint one of his landscapes live there within 30 minutes. Every ten minutes the camera panned over to him and showed the progress. They were all amazed by his skills. But there were no follow-up appearances. He also took part in a casting and was very impressive, but here too without any tangible results. Our "Happy Painter" was devastated, once again. So he carried on as usual. Painting in the shopping center, selling paintings from the VW bus, lessons. But then, in late autumn, his agent called him: "Bill, have you heard that a new TV station has opened? They're called KOCE-TV,[36] over in Huntington Beach. And they're looking for something new for their educational program." 21 years after William emigrated, this phone call would finally herald his big breakthrough. An appointment was made and William packed up all his paintings. They were even piled up on the passenger seat. He was determined not to waste this opportunity.

He then met with his agent on the TV station premises. The 58-year-old William liked it here immediately. There were young TV people scurrying around everywhere and everything seemed so dynamic and so positive to him. "Fire in," he shouted, clenching his fist. William put as many paintings as he could carry under his agent's arms, and he juggled the rest - it was still a huge pile - into the station manager's office himself. William later recalled and said that the young station manager, his name was Don Gerdts, with his black hair and mustache and goatee, looked as if he could play the villain in any Errol Flynn film.[37] But Gerdts was a fine guy who had every single picture of William shown to him and himself listened to everything patiently. After showing his paintings, Gerdts asked him if he could really create such paintings in just 30 minutes. "You bet," William replied, grinning. Don

Gerdts leaned back behind his desk and thought for a while. For William it felt like an eternity. Then he leaned forward again and pointed at William: "Do you know, Mr. Alexander, what we are doing? We'll shoot a pilot film with you. You paint an oil painting in 30 minutes in front of the camera, and then we see whether the audience likes it. We're a new TV station, we don't have any money, so we can't pay you anything for this pilot. But if it works, we'll do a season and then earn something. Is that okay with you?" William beamed and immediately agreed. When he asked if he had an audience, Gerdts declined because it would cost money. Only William, his easel and the camera would be in the studio. The thought of being in the studio with only one camera suddenly made William uneasy. He was used to communicating with the audience and involving them. Don Gerdts abruptly brought him out of his thoughts and asked what he wanted to earn if there was a season? William smiled: "Give me what I'm worth and what's fair." That's how it should be, and Don Gerdts has always proven to be fair, very fair in fact, over the years.

His easel was then set up in the studio and the camera was positioned. The production manager, a Mr. Greene, and William both didn't really know how to start. Together with the cameraman they first looked at what perspectives they wanted to work from, and William started to sweat. If there was an audience, he could play with them and everything would be very easy. But here it was just him alone. It was decided that William should just start, initially without a camera. And William started, just like he always did in the shopping centers. He slammed the brush on the canvas and moved wildly back and forth until Mr. Greene interrupted him: „No no, no, Mr. Alexander. You're not allowed to move around too much. You have to stand still. Don't move too much, please." Then he gave the signal for the recording to begin. All the spotlights came on and the temperature in the small studio rose noticeably. William started sweating even more, also from nervousness. What was he supposed to say? Where should he look? And then he also had to remember that he wasn't allowed to move too much. "Camera on," he heard Mr. Greene call, and the camera, less than two meters from William, suddenly flashed red. William in his distress imagined all his friends and students sitting around him, it gave him mental strength, and he looked straight into the camera: "Hello, my name is Bill Alexander, and I can teach you how to paint." Then he started painting and talking, just like he did in front of his students. When the recording ended, he felt awful. It had all gone terribly, he said. The timing was wrong, and then his terrible German accent. That was all nothing. He drove home disappointed and didn't hear anything from the TV station for a while. So Anna Margarete and he went their usual way. He painted in the shopping areas, gave lessons and sold his paintings from his VW bus. Meanwhile, the TV station had broadcast the pilot film with William. Following the film, the television audience was asked whether they liked it and whether they wanted to see more of it. The response was amazing. Within a few days, the station received 200 calls and 150 letters. So far, the station has only received this many responses in the course of an entire year. The audience response was clear: they all wanted to see William! Don Gerdts called him immediately, it was the middle of the night, and the slightly sleepy William was suddenly wide awake after a few words from Gerdts. The management of PBS, a network of various TV stations that also included KOCE, wanted to film a season with William. The title was also born: "The Magic of Oil Painting." The title was fitting because what happened on the canvas was like magic. William should come to the studio as quick as possible. Now his life took on a whole new dynamic; now he would be able to teach students all over the country. PBS had 120 affiliates, which was an audience of millions. But not all broadcasters wanted to show William initially. A PBS station in Chicago originally did not want to air the show because the station manager found William's German accent and awkward manner in front of the camera intolerable. Because of the great success of "The Magic of Oil Painting" he quickly changed his mind. William had half an hour, and he perfected his timing. From then on he needed exactly 27 minutes and 40 seconds for his painting. He quickly learned how to interact with the TV audience and always used the recording time to convey his worldview in addition to all the tips and tricks he brought to the audience. The positive thinking, the goal of a happy life, a life with mother nature and the belief in a better tomorrow. All of that was always included. In a 1983 interview in the Los Angeles Times, Don Gerdts said of William: What Alexander does is painting, but he sells a philosophy of life. And his philosophy is: Don't be afraid to try new and different things. He makes you want to do it. That's his mystique." His popularity grew quickly. Over the years he received more and more fan mail. In the end, five employees were accommodated in a caravan during the filming days in order to answer the 2,000 fan letters every week from there. There were countless letters of thanks for all the inspiration, but also declarations of love. And William answered many a letter himself. One letter remained in his memory for a long time, and he had to laugh so hard about it. A guy from Alabama wrote at him and said he had been trying to paint trees for years just like William showed on TV. But they all looked lousy and he was about to give up. But then, like William, he decided to talk while painting. Actually, the trees have gotten a little better. And the guy from Alabama said that he then copied William's terrible accent when he spoke. And lo and behold, it worked! His trees suddenly looked really good. He concluded the letter with the joking words: "Now I know your secret."

The first episode of season one flickered on the TV screens on February 18, 1974. 13 episodes were planned per season, and one 30-minute episode ran per week. The last episode of the first season was seen on May 13, 1974. The team then had enough time to produce the next season, which would run from February to May of the following year. Nine seasons were filmed, a total of 117 episodes. Ultimately, 120 PBS stations broadcast his show. The last broadcast was on the 10th. May 1982. Once the ball started rolling, things became easier for William. Much easier! An acquaintance of his was the book publisher Walter Foster, who had already brought several art books onto the market that explained painting step by step to the reader. He had never asked William if he would like to do a book with him. But after Williams' popularity rose through the TV show, Mr. Foster suddenly approached him. And it was a win-win situation. Everyone benefited. The broadcaster, the publisher, and of course William. The book became a bestseller. Other bestsellers followed. William reached his peak, he even made an appearance on Johnny Carson's legendary "Tonight Show."[38] He was recognized in public and he was constantly surrounded by his fans.

Privately, he was a person like everyone else. He had his little pet peeves and bad habits too. But he always thought positively, the glass was always half full for him. He couldn't stand it when there was negative energy around him. And when such people were around him, he quickly withdrew from them. He also had many crazy ideas that cost him dearly. He was just an artist, and money gave him the freedom to express himself, even if the money was usually spent very rashly. When one of his ideas flopped, he would laugh heartily and then just say that he just wanted to show how not to do it. Bill wasn't particularly educated, and he knew it. After all, he had only been to elementary school in East Prussia. So he respected "educated people" because he knew he wasn't. But he was as clever as a fox, he always said, and he was a rascal. He was also an idealist. Mostly he just believed that if you went through life with good intentions, good things would just happen. But life is different, more complex, people have different natures, he didn't always understand that. He truly believed in making the world a better place. He really wanted to encourage others to do the same. William, who loved being called "Bill," was and always wanted to be a good guy. He always had good intentions and was always very generous, often to his own detriment because not everyone around him was decent. Bill wasn't very well read and mostly only knew what was happening in the world from the radio and television news. But he had clear views, especially when it came to war. He himself had to gain the most extensive experience. But he only talked about it in very close circles, usually over coffee or his fish breakfast. And although he was against the war, he didn't always seem like a pacifist, which he was. William could quickly become angry and find clear words when bad or unscrupulous policies were being made. He knew money meant power. And power corrupts. When Mikhail Gorbachev[39] once came to Vancouver for a conference, William drove there with his foster son just to hear him speak.Gorbachev became a hero in his eyes when the Cold War[40] came to an end. He advocated for peace and understanding, and William saw a better world coming for people. In this context, he gave Gorbachev one of his paintings as a gift.

„The Magic of Oil Painting"

Here is the chronological list of the individual episodes
with the respective first broadcast date:

Season 1

- A Morning Kind of Mountain
  (18. February 1974)
- After the Storm (25. February 1974)
- Along the Moulon Rouge (4. March 1974)
- Autumn Lake (11. March 1974)
- Canadian Canyon (18. March 1974)
- Country Road (25. March 1974)
- Glacier Bay (1. April 1974)
- Green Rain Forest (8. April 1974)
- Hillgrueber's Farm (15. April 1974)
- Mountain Island (22. April 1974)
- Rain (29. April 1974)
- Solitude (6. May 1974)
- Winter Shack (13. May 1974)

Season 2

- Alpine Junction (17. February 1975)
- Craggy Pass (24. February 1975)
- Candle on Black (3. March 1975)
- Frozen Citadel (10. March 1975)
- Looking for Gold (17. March 1975)
- Miller's Colony (24. March 1975)
- Mountain River (31. March 1975)
- Mountain Road (7. April 1975)
- Mr. Brown's Farm (14. April 1975)
- Neptunes Bateau (21. April 1975)
- Silver Plume Lake (28. April 1975)
- Steel Lake (5. May 1975)
- Autumn Colors (12. May 1975)

Season 3

- Along the Swan River (16. February 1976)
- Autumn Dream (February 23, 1976)
- Beyond the Arctic Circle (1. March 1976)
- Columbia River Gorge (8. March 1976)
- Fall River (15. March 1976)
- Haystack Rock (22. March 1976)
- Holiday Mountain (29. March 1976)
- Mountain Water Runoff (5. April 1976)
- Seascape (12. April 1976)
- The Homestead (19. April 1976)
- To The Summit (26. April 1976)
- Vase by Knife (3. May 1976)
- Waterfall and Rapids (10. May 1976)

Season 4

- Alpine Lagoon (21. February 1977)
- At The Beach (28. February 1977)
- Bills Covered Bridge (7. March 1977)
- Black Canvas Still Life (14. March 1977)
- City Silhouette (21. March 1977)
- Don't Fence Me In (28. March 1977)
- Grand Canyon (4. April 1977)
- Lake Kabetogama (11. April 1977)
- Midnight Roses (18. April 1977)
- Sunset I (25. April 1977)
- Sylvan Path (2. May 1977)
- Texas Scene (9. May 1977)
- Thousand Island Lake (16. May 1977)

Season 5
- Colorado River Canyon (20. February 1978)
- Desert Canyon (27. February 1978)
- Falling Leaves (6. March 1978)
- Falling Water (13. March 1978)
- Grapes and a Jug II (20. March 1978)
- Greener Pastures (27. March 1978)
- Knife Mountain (3. April 1978)
- Mountain Lake and Island (10. April 1978)
- Near Lassen CA (17. April 1978)
- Red Sailboat (24. April 1978)
- Still Life in Vase (1. May 1978)
- Stormy Ocean (8. May 1978)
- Swamp Two (15. May 1978)

Season 6
- Candle on Black (19. February 1979)
- Fall Touches (26. February 1979)
- Lower Falls I (5. March 1979)
- Montana de Oro (12. March 1979)
- Natures Bounty (19. March 1979)
- Rolling Mist (26. March 1979)
- Sunset Beach (2. April 1979)
- Tumalo Trail (9. April 1979)
- Western Skies (16. April 1979)
- West Virginia Mountains (23. April 1979)
- Winter Day (30. April 1979)
- Winter Lake (6. May 1979)
- Winter Scene (13. May, 1979)

Season 7
- Adirondack Pleasure (18. February 1980)
- Apple Valley (25. February 1980)
- Autumn Dreams (3. March 1980)
- Evening At Eagle Lake (10. March 1980)
- Grand Marais Pines (17. March 1980)
- Lac du Flambeau (24. March 1980)

- Merced River Yosemite (31. March 1980)
- Moonlight Mirage (7. April 1980)
- Secluded Cabin (14. April 1980)
- Snowy Mountain Road (21. April 1980)
- Still Life and Grapefruit (28. April 1980)
- Sunlight I (5. May 1980)
- West Virginia River (12. May 1980)

Season 8
- Bill's Mountain Waterfall (16. February 1981)
- Dell's Pond (23. February 1981)
- Down By The Riverside (2. March 1981)
- Forest Hollow (9. March 1981)
- Gorgeous Gorge (16. March 1981)
- Island Eve (23. March 1981)
- Jeffrey Pine (30. March 1981)
- Marigold on Black (6. April 1981)
- Mountain in the Clouds (13. April 1981)
- Mount Baker (20. April 1981)
- Quetico Wilderness (27. April 1981)
- Rain Forest (4. May 1981)
- Robin Hood Bay (11. May 1981)

Season 9
- Big Mountain (15. February 1982)
- Butterfly (22. February 1982)
- Daisies with a Knife (1. March 1982)
- Farm Scene (8. March 1982)
- Hidden Falls (15. March 1982)
- Jar Still Life (22. March 1982)
- Lonely Pine (29. March 1982)
- Lost Lagoon (5. April 1982)
- Moonlit Splendor (12. April 1982)
- Mountain Paradise (19. April 1982)
- Silver Falls (26. April 1982)
- The Wall (3. May 1982)
- Winter Sky (10. May 1982)

Paradise at the end of Highway 101

When they weren't in Los Angeles for studio work or because William was teaching classes to ever-larger groups, both of them were still looking for a home surrounded by nature where they could realize their dream of independent living. Then in 1975 they found it. In British Columbia, at the end of Highway 101, in Powell River. To get to this place you had to leave your car at the end of the highway and take two different ferries. That was exactly how William liked it. They had basically reached the end of the world. He later jokingly wrote that Moses wandered in the desert for 40 years until the promised land came into view. It took him, William, 60 years to do it. In Powell River the nature lover found everything that pleased him. The sea was close, the high mountains in the background wore white caps of snow, the forests and meadows were lush. There were rivers and lakes everywhere and the climate was mild. Each season had its own charm and its own magic. William looked around with his girlfriend to see if there was a piece of land to buy somewhere here. There was some on the coast, but the prices were astronomical. Prices were cheaper in the interior of the country, but no one wanted to sell here at the moment. Both were frustrated and feared that this dream would be shattered again before it even began. Then they received the tip that they should drive to a certain property. The owner there, an old Norwegian named Olav Amundsen, has been wanting to sell for a long time. His wife died some time ago and his children had long since left the house. The two immediately drove to the property described to get to know the old Norwegian. Olav Amundsen could have starred in any Viking film. He was an old, gnarled man with bright eyes that he could narrow into small slits with which he would then stare at you with razor sharpness. The hard life he led left endless wrinkles, no, pardon, runes, on his face. But he had a friendly and warm personality. The property of the Norwegian was beautiful. It was on the edge of the forest, firs and cedars grew there, and the high mountains could be seen in the background. Behind his house there was a river in which salmon swam. The house, however, was the shabby and run-down house that the two of them had ever seen. It was ripe for demolition. But that didn't deter the two of them. Here was their paradise, they felt it. William asked what he wanted, and the Norwegian said they could get anything for a little money. He dreams of driving through the country in a motorhome and wanting to see everything he didn't yet know. This is how he wants to end his life. They reached a trade agreement. Well, the next big adventure can now begin. First Anna Margarete and Wilhelm had to prepare the property. There were countless stones and boulders lying around on the partly rocky ground. Removing them was a real challenge. It took a while, but they got them all away except one. It was so big and heavy that it had to stay, but they would find a use for it. After all the weed and bushes were torn out, you could plan your paradise. First they would build a beautiful two-story wooden house with a large roof terrace. Since there was currently no electricity connection on the property, our "Happy Painter" had to dig a trench in the rocky ground from the house down to the street. It was a killing spree. But little by little everything came into being. The two planted vines around the huge rock near the house. All the neighbors laughed at first and said that wine doesn't grow on the ground here. But they were wrong; the largest and sweetest grapes grew far and wide. The rock radiated so much heat that the vines felt right at home there. After the house met their wishes, they dug a large pond directly opposite and also drilled a well. Anna Margarete planted fir and cedar trees around the new pond and the entire area was lovingly designed. However, the river behind the house proved to be a bit treacherous. The salmon swam there, but at spawning time there was a bad smell behind the house because then the already dead fish floated up there with their bellies up. William saw itpragmatically and stoically fished them all out. He dug deep holes around the newly planted trees and buried the salmon there. The trees thrived! William then built his studio opposite their house, followed by work sheds and a large chicken coop with an enclosure. It was a real small farm. They had geese, ducks, chickens and fish. A lovely dog named "Brandy" also found his home there. As long as they lived in Powell River, William had many plans. He wanted to gradually acquire more land and build a bird park. He was a pioneer in many things. He who loved Mother Nature so much, he now wanted to give her something back. For example, he set up a fish farm; salmon were to be bred on a large scale and then released into the wild. And in fact, up to 40,000 salmon were released into the rivers every year. William spent tens of thousands of dollars on his projects, a small fortune at the time. Since William still loved fishing so much, it was only natural that he would get a seaworthy boat. Everyone there had a boat, because if you didn't have one, the only way to get across to Vancouver Island was to use the public ferries. Powell River also had another advantage. After Bill became more and more famous, more and more of his fans tried to find his address. Some people did it and Anna Margarete then had to slip into the spontaneous role of host from one moment to the next, which she absolutely disliked. Powell River, at the end of the world, was ideal. His foster son once reported that it took him more than eleven hours to get from his home in Port Alberni to Powell River, a distance of around 150 kilometers, so that from then on they preferred to only meet in Vancouver.

Things were going well for William in his life now. Only the sales of his paints and brushes left something to be desired. He had found various manufacturers based in Montreal and Toronto who produced according to his wishes. He even had a patent for his painting knife. One evening the phone rang and a certain Sid Knudsen was on the other end. Knudsen's wife recently attended one of William's classes and hasI somehow noticed William saying something about the slow sales of his brushes. She told her husband, who was immediately hooked. Sid Knudsen has worked in all kinds of industries. He was a trucker on the West Coast, a lumberjack and a steelworker. Now he wanted to change his career again and selling painting supplies sounded very good and exciting to him. Sid could organize and speak well. So he offered himself to William. He listened patiently to the explanations on the phone. But he was reserved. Since he achieved a certain level of fame, many people have offered themselves to him, and not all of them had good intentions. He also noticed changes in his circle of friends, some of which hurt him greatly. William could indulge. Envy and resentment were completely alien to him. But it happened repeatedly that old companions, mostly artists who had not yet achieved a breakthrough, asked with envy and resentment why he of all people made it and not they themselves. These experiences taught him a certain caution. Then William asked the man on the phone if he thought the brush sale should be combined with the show. He got a long silence in response, and then Sid asked what kind of show he was talking about. William understood and laughed at himself." Just because I have a show on television doesn't mean that everyone has to know me." William was really relieved. The man on the phone didn't even know he was famous. He immediately had a good feeling and invited Sid and his wife to Powell River. A few days later they met. William was wearing one of his old jackets and his beloved sailor's hat. William could have gone fishing or woodcutting. Sid Knudsen, on the other hand, wore a brown suit and looked perfectly dressed. Sid was tall and looked strikingly similar to the Hollywood star Robert Ryan[41] (this actor is now only known to middleaged, cinematic readers, among other things through his role as Captain Nemo or through westerns such as "The Feared Four"). William and his visitor quickly realized that they liked each other, and they quickly agreed that Sid would from now on take care of the marketing of paints, canvases and brushes. He even took out a mortgage on his house and founded a company based in Salem, Oregon. Time passed, William heard little from Sid, until one evening Sid suddenly contacted him: "William, this is Sid, the man with the brown suit." They both had to laugh, and the saying "the man with that brown suit" became a running joke for you from then on. "I hope you're sitting down, because I have big news. I got a major customer, the Aaron Brothers company!" This company was one of the major art supply companies with 55 stores in several states. From now on, the entire range should be available in all branches. Over time, Sid became a good friend and even William's manager in the end.

In 1979, major changes were underway at the local station KOCE. A new studio director was hired. Carrol Ellerbe. A well-known professional who was previously at NBC and who has won several Emmy Awards[42] with his spectacular productions. First and foremost, he wanted to take special care of William and "The Magic of Oil Painting." When William found out this, he felt a little uneasy in his stomach and secretly feared that the new director would find him, the emigrant with the terrible accent, clumsy. But nothing like that happened. Mr. Ellerbe wanted to make the production more elegant and not as static as before. "William, we'll change things for you with the cameras. Just imagine us dancing together here. They lead and we always follow. Move. Just do whatever you want, and we'll always be on your heels." William breathed a sigh of relief and later described how working with the cameramen was actually much more relaxed from then on. There was a lot more laughter and a lot more joking around. If you look at some old episodes and compare them with those that have now been filmed, the newer ones are much more varied and smoother in terms of editing. There are various different perspectives, close-up shots, and it is repeatedly noticeable that William, in his dynamic acting, always has to subtly look at which camera is pointed at him. And the efforts paid off. In 1979, William's show received the coveted „Emmy Award." Sid Knudsen, „the man with the brown suit," continued to demonstrate his marketing talent. When he wasn't filming, he organized sales tours in major shopping centers across the country with William as the main attraction. He also expanded the business and, together with William, expanded the product range; after all, it was all about selling paints and brushes. The first few seasons had William on a black screen every now and then painted. To do this, a white canvas was first primed with matt latex paint. Since the slow-drying "Magic White" only works on white canvases, William then primed these black canvases with any other color, blue or green for example. It just had to be transparent, that is, not opaque. He applied this color exactly the same as the "Magic White," and it also fulfills roughly the same function. With the caveat, perhaps, that if you choose a green shade, for example, all subsequent shades will be mixed with green, which limits the color. That's why they came up with a counterpart to „Magic White," the „Clear Vanish," which also dried slowly. Now all colors could be used on the black canvas, which enabled a completely new play of colors. A variety of special brushes followed over the years. Business was going well. Although William wasn't particularly interested in the business content, that was Sid's business. He spoke to the manufacturers and producers about what his products should be like and otherwise concentrated on his show and the instruction.

Incidentally, William was not a co-owner of the newly founded company. But everything was precisely regulated. For every article produced with his name or image, he received predetermined royalties from Sid Knudsen. William also had a personal service agreement with KOCE-TV, which continued to produce, sell and broadcast his programs. This earned him about $40,000 annually. So his sources of income came mainly from his contract with the television station, then from the royalties from the sale of the art supplies, and partly from paintings that he may have sold. Everything was very relaxed, especially with Sid, with whom an increasingly close friendship developed. It must have been around the mid-1980s when KOCE-TV suddenly gave William an assistant, to put it charmingly. This assistant was always at his side when William came to Los Angeles to film. She was a kind of "chaperone," which sounds much nicer than the more accurate term "guardian," who had to make sure that William always got to where he was supposed to be. Because time and time again he came either too early, or too late, or not at all because he was waiting somewhere else. He sometimes seemed like such a dreamy and distracted professor. During filming in Los Angeles, she "looked after him constantly." Because William had already been attacked twice in the city when he went out alone. He could be very naive and a bit "helpless," to use the words of his foster son. Although this was a very endearing and human quality of William's, it was also quite dangerous for him if he was in the wrong place at the wrong time.

William Alexander and his student Bob Ross

One of the many millions of viewers of Williams' show was in Alaska. He was originally from Florida, but had committed to the Air Force for 20 years and was at some point transferred to the far north. His name was Bob Ross. He had a son named Steve from his first marriage, but his parents separated and so he married a second time. Bob used every free minute to paint. Landscapes were his thing, but he wasn't that good at painting portraits, as he confessed to a presenter years later. But he loved nature, as did William. Ross was fascinated by how quickly and easily William created his landscapes. In an interview he once said: "I saw Alexander on TV. Like millions of other people. I was inspired, learned from him, and when I got out of the military, they offered me a job as an art teacher."[43] And that's how it was. He initially took part in a course taught by William. That wasn't so easy anymore, because William's courses had long been so popular that there were long waiting times. But he was lucky and got a place. William quickly became aware of the talented young man and took him on. At some point the idea arose to train an art teacher in order to meet the ever-increasing demand for painting courses and workshops as a whole. Ross's military service ended on July 31, 1981, and he set out to become a painting teacher. At William's he was supposed to carry the „Alexander Technique," as it was called in advertising, to the people like an evangelism, conduct courses and thereby sell the products of his line of „Magic" paint products tailored to this painting technique locally. There is a photograph from 1982. William had one of his performances at the legendary Woodfield Shopping Center in Chicago. Thousands of people sat around his stage and William moderated. In the background on the stage, his newly hired "instructor" Bob stood at the easel and painted. There is also a little anecdote. When William was taken from his small waiting room by an assistant and brought to the stage, so many fans, mostly female, rushed towards him that several police officers had to surround him and bring him onto the stage. William felt like a felon and then joked with the audience: „No, no, I didn't do anything wrong, I really didn't steal anything." The audience laughed, even the police officers, involuntarily integrated into the show, were able to smile don't resist. At the end of his training, Ross was specifically prepared for future work at the headquarters of Sid Knudsen's company in Salem (Oregon). Then finally he was able to act as the "Happy Painter's Instructor" to get started. The life of a traveling art teacher was anything but easy. He traveled with his luggage for about eight months of the year. Before he came to a city, advertisements were placed in the newspapers, and he then showed up on a certain date in a cheap hotel ballroom, in a community center, a church or even in one of the countless corner shops. He then set up his workplace there and collected the course fee, which was between 20-30 dollars per person, sold his painting supplies and then gave the workshop. Sometimes he stayed for a day and moved on, sometimes longer courses were offered. Ross had long mastered the basics of the "Alexander Technique," but now it was time to master the presentation as well. William expected his master student to use the same sayings as he did, and just as dynamically and enthusiastically as he did. William regularly used terms in his shows such as: "Funny little trees" or "happy little things." Also the term "almighty " was used constantly and in all variations, and the audience liked it. He spoke of the "almighty painting knife" as well as the "almighty artist" or "almighty pictures." But the most well-known was probably his saying: "Fire in!" He clenched his fist and you could feel that William had more energy than him the sun seemed to have. Although his student did most of the "happy" sayings, his voice was gentle and quiet. A journalist once called it: "Encouragement through purring self-affirmation." He left out the aggressive "Fire in," but instead created a different play on words. Ross called himself, in Allusion to the "Happy Painter," often "The Happy Alaskan." This nickname initially caught on, but by 1984 he had adopted the nickname "Happy Painter," as newspaper advertisements show. At first he was completely absorbed in his role, and in one of his coloring books Ross later wrote this dedication to his teacher: "In a time when it is said that there are no heroes, I feel very lucky to have a giant in the field to have been

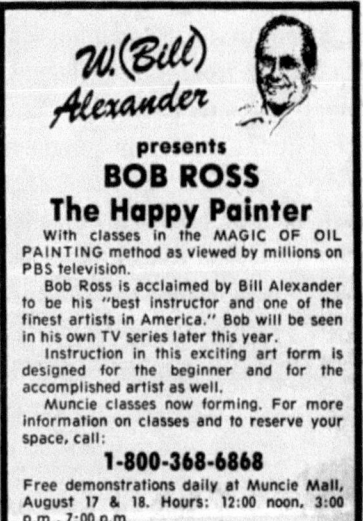

While in the ad above, probably from 1982, Bob Ross was announced as "The Happy Painter's Instructor," in 1984 he is presented as "The Happy Painter" (photo on the right).

inspired and influenced by art – Bill Alexander. He was my mentor and friend and was so instrumental in everything I achieved." The situation changed dramatically when Annette Kowalski appeared in one of the painting classes. Her son passed away a year before, and Ross kind of inspired her. They got to know each other and she advised him to start his own business. Her husband and she would actively support him. The idea was to basically adopt William's concept. Lessons and workshops in front of paying students combined with the sale of all kinds of painting supplies.

The Kowalski and Ross couples founded a joint company in 1985. Each of the four partners held 25% of the company, and to save money, the Ross family even moved in with the Kowalskis in the early days. His son Steve later reported that his father even had a temporary relationship with Annette.[44] The business partners also saw their future on television in order to generate more customers. "Ross had begun teaching his own wet-on-wet classes, and a cohort of students and PBS leaders took notice. His approach to painting was the same as Alexander's, but his temperament was different. Instead of being excited, Ross was fascinatingly calm and had a gentle, lilting voice. His gaze was also familiar and approachable; He wore worn jeans, flannel shirts, and a skirt reminiscent of 1970s hippie culture. People loved him not only for his skillful painting skills, but also for his ability to calm them. In 1983, PBS replaced Alexander's show with „The Joy of Painting," hosted by Ross."[45] The film was shot in the kitchen of a private home, which was hung in black. In just under 30 minutes he painted a complete landscape in front of the camera. PBS also came up with a very special advertisement for "The Joy of Painting." On September 21, 1982, a TV commercial was broadcast showing William Alexander and Ross next to each other. William hands his paintbrush to him, almost like a torch.[46] "I hand my mighty brush to a mighty man, and that is Bob Ross," exclaimed Alexander. „Thank you, Bill," Ross replied with typical calm. In the first season, Ross said about his teacher William: "It almost made me angry when I saw Alexander on TV for the first time that he could do in a few minutes what took me days." In the first episode of the second season of "The Joy of Painting," Ross once again paid tribute to Alexander, saying, "Years ago, Bill taught me this fantastic technique, and I feel like he gave me a precious gift." I want that gift would be happy to share with you."[47] From then on, a local station in the PBS network produced "The Joy of Painting." From 1983 to 1994, a total of 31 seasons with 13 episodes each were filmed. On average there were three seasons a year. During William Alexander in North America reached an audience of millions and was able to present his "Alexander painting technique", it was Bob Ross who showed this painting technique to an audience around the globe. His series was broadcast in around 30 countries worldwide. Millions of people were and are still inspired by its consequences and encouraged to paint with the "Alexandrian painting technique." The New York Times wrote in a December 22, 1991 article on page 33: "As popular as the television show may be, it is the smallest blot on the canvas of Mr. Ross's $15 million, Orlando-based empire -Industry of guides, videos and especially Bob Ross art supplies. There are more than 300 certified Bob Ross instructors (his son Steven, 24, is one) and more than a million amateur Bob Ross painters, all creating remarkably similar landscapes of snow-capped mountains, shimmering lakes and windswept trees, Artworks with titles such as "Autumn Fantasy," "Southwest Serenity," and "Waterfall Won-der." Over the years, however, the relationship between the four business partners cooled drastically. Ross valued the best quality of paints and brushes, the Kowalskis valued sales, which Ross increasingly suffered from. His old friend and fellow artist John Thamm[48] later said in an interview: "I sometimes wonder how everything would have turned out if he hadn't gotten involved with Annette and Walt Kowalski. Maybe things would have turned out better for him."

Meanwhile, in 1983, KOCE honored William by publishing his memoirs, "The Bill Alexander Story. An Autobiography by W. Alexander." He dedicated this book to his daughter Heidi, then Christine, who was the daughter of Anna Margarete from a previous relationship and Stan. Stan(islav), that is Talore's birth name. But William didn't disappear from the TV stage. He continued to appear in painting shows. As early as 1982, episodes of the program "William Alexander - Magic Art Instructor" ran on PBS, continuing the same concept as "The Magic of Oil Painting." One-hour painting programs were even produced with him. From 1984 to 1992, William appeared in the series "The Art of Bill Alexander and Robert Warren" on PBS. The artists took turns painting in each episode. New artists were also continually added to William's side, with the name of the new artist appearing in the title. In keeping with the series, besliding books created. The relationship between William and his former student also cooled noticeably over time and a rather competitive relationship emerged, as can be read in an article:[49] "Eventually Mr. Ross found an art teacher in California who gave him was able to demonstrate exactly how to paint a tree using the quick, foolproof "wet-on-wet" method. "I took a course and went crazy," he said. "I knew it was what I wanted to do." Mr. Ross eventually founded his own traveling art school in Florida. In 1982 his company took off. He refused to name the teacher who first inspired him, explaining somewhat uneasily: "Now he is our main competitor. In fact, the rivalry between Mr. Ross and his former mentor William Alexander is bitter. Mr. Alexander, 76, ..., who has his own painting show on a public television station in Orange County, Calif., also has a paint supply store and a line of books and videos. He spoke about his former protégé in the tones that Thomas Couture would have used to describe the young student who overtook him, Edouard Manet. "He betrayed me," he

(William Alexander) said in his thick German accent. "I invented "wet on wet." I trained him and he copies me - what bothers me is not only that he cheated on me, but also that he thinks he can do better."[50]

As part of the research and the countless conversations I had in advance, it quickly became apparent that even today, among those who know both Alexander and Ross, there is still a very passionate discussion about who is the more important artist the two of them. I think everyone should answer this question for themselves. Ross learned the "Alexander Mat Technique" and spread it around the globe through television. He could paint landscapes and, as we have already heard, he was not good at portraiture. William Alexander, on the other hand, was the inventor of this painting technique. He was also very good at taking portraits and creating still lifes. His creative palette was much more complex, I think. Finally, as we will find out shortly, he also knew how to create elaborate political allegories. To do this, the artist needs much more than just an understanding of colors or talent in image composition. Here, sophisticated statements are developed and transferred to the canvas in a painterly manner. This is undoubtedly a completely different artistic league. The following passage in the aforementioned article in the New York Times is also informative on this topic: ... "Mr. Ross, who claims to have created almost 30,000 paintings (the prolific Picasso did not achieve this record), does not sell his paintings and does not show his works in galleries; He only had one retrospective - at the Minnetrista Cultural Center in Muncie, a city that prides itself on calling the artist an honorary son of the locals. Mr. Ross said he had no desire for a large exhibition. „There are thousands of very, very talented artists who will never be known, even if they are dead," he said. "Most painters want recognition, especially from their colleagues. I achieved that a long time ago with television. That's all I need." This view was reflected somewhat more sourly in New York City. „People definitely know who he is," said Kevin Lavin, 38, a struggling painter. „In his own way, he's as famous as Warhol," he added with a pained look. Mr. Lavin, who works at the Pearl Paint Company, a large art supply store in the SoHo neighborhood of Manhattan, pointed to the store's display of Bob Ross items and said mockingly, „That's Bob's happy little corner." The 3rd $56 tubes of Prussian blue and sap green, each embossed with Bob Ross's name and likeness, were stored in a dusty back section, a safe distance from the gleaming rows of oil paints and supplies used by regulars . „We hide them," Mr. Lavin said of Bob Ross' products, „so as not to offend." Mr. Lavin looked for a bright side. „I suppose in a way he brought a lot of people with him who wouldn't normally be involved in art," he said cautiously. But is it art? „It's carpentry," said fellow sculptor Keith Frank. „It's formulaic and thoughtless, ,art as therapy.'" They described the Bob Ross style as „pizzeria art," paintings that were often hung in pizzerias. Like many famous artists, Mr.

Ross is not entirely loved by his peers. „I'm appalled by the art classes on television," said Richard PousetteDart, an abstract expressionist who teaches at the Students Art League in New York. "It's terrible, bad, bad, bad. They're just commercial exploiters, non-artists teaching other non-artists." He added, „I don't teach technique or method, I encourage students to find their own." But Mr. Ross listens did not respond to his critics and said he had no desire for acceptance in the contemporary art world."

I would like to point out at this point that no verifiable evidence has been discovered that Ross actually created 30,000 works in his life, but I don't necessarily want to doubt that. What is at least certain is that he created each motif that he painted in his TV show a total of three times. A picture was painted as a draft before the broadcast, then the painting followed during the broadcast, and finally he painted a more developed version again for later marketing. With 403 episodes, you would get 1209 documented paintings that are said to still be in the company's storage rooms today.

The drama begins

Bill and Anna Margarete lived in Powell River in harmony with nature. They got up early and looked after all their animals. The chickens finally demanded their grain, the fish in the pond wanted to be fed by William, and their dog Brandy loved to chase the geese around the pond. But when the geese got together, it was Brandy who had to escape. Every year at Christmas, Bill made it a point to bring one of the geese to the Christmas dinner table. But every year when the time came, in the end he couldn't bring himself to do it. And so the geese community grew steadily. Another character that we still have to pay attention to was the Chinese rooster Napoleon. He was black with red spots, a great guy, and he was the boss of the chicken run. He took his job of protecting the chickens from all harm very seriously. This was also the case the day an eagle attacked. He heroically threw himself against the robber. Anna Margarete saw it from the house and immediately ran over. But too late, the eagle flew away and the faithful Napoleon lay crumpled on the ground, he had to give up a lot of things and maybe even his life in the end. All the chickens were running back and forth excitedly, it was a complete chaos, but Margarete was astonished when she noticed that not a single chicken was missing. The loyal Napoleon had actually driven away the eagle. And this intrepid, shattered fellow also picked himself up again after a few minutes. He was pretty badly damaged and it took a few days until he was fit again, and he had been limping on one leg ever since. But he was the hero of the day, and his limp only made him all the more interesting to the chickens. Bill regularly went out to sea in his small fishing boat to fish. Anna Margarete was always afraid for him, especially when the waves were a little higher and a storm was approaching. But Bill always just laughed and said that he usually catches the fish and eats them. But if he were to sink, the fish would eat him. That is more than just fair. But at some point his boat became too small for him. He wanted to have a real fishing boat. A big boat, a custom "Alexander creation." So he grabbed a drawing pad and designed his dream boat. Bill had some buddies on site who would help him with the construction. One knew how to build boats. His name was „Wally," and he also emigrated from Germany in 1951. He came from Lörrach. The other guy knew how to make rigging. The next guy worked on engines and the youngest of them all, the poor guy, ended up having to do the physical work. William was the boss and was always busy running back and forth. Most of the time, however, he just stopped the others from working because something new came to his mind. The new fishing boat was around eight meters long and was intended to be a professional fishing boat. And he even applied for an official fishing license. All the fun probably cost him well over $15,000 in the end. But the whole story once again had a catch, because something went terribly wrong during the planning. In the end, this boat was completely unseaworthy. Even the slightest wave would probably have caused the unstable boat to capsize. William never went fishing on the open sea in the boat he named "Magic." They repeatedly tried to somehow save the boat, but at some point he admitted the fiasco and sold it to the local metal dealer... at the current price for scrap per kilo.[51] Anna Margarete was beside herself that he had made a fortune again had sunk it, but Bill just smiled mildly and said: "It was money happily earned, you can also spend it happily, no one was harmed." So when he wasn't fishing or in his studio painting, then He repaired some fences, the chimney or dragged a dead log from the forest that he wanted to carve one day. They also traveled a lot around the country. Bill loved these "road trips," where you just drove along and stopped wherever you wanted. And whenever he discovered an idyllic river or lake, the first thing he did was get the fishing rods out. Anna Margarete knew it well enough and sat down under a tree with a book and a cigarette. So they got older, and William began to notice some abnormalities. So it happened more and more often that his concentration waned and he became increasingly easily distracted by all sorts of things. It happened several times that he went to the shopping center with Anna Margarete, and while she went to the food department, William strolled into this department and that department. He was like a butterfly flying from flower to flower. And when he picked out a pack of nails in the tool department, he suddenly remembered that he would also need beams. So he drove straight from the shopping center to the wood shop, bought beams and boards, and then immediately brought them home without realizing that he had forgotten his partner in the shopping center. She then repeatedly had to take a taxi home with everything packed. Something like this and more like it happened more and more often, and the first small cracks began to appear in their relationship. In one of his TV shows in 1991, Bill described a similar incident in a shopping center. Whenever people come towards him whistling contentedly, he becomes curious and follows them. Just to see what kind of person he is, maybe even to start a conversation with him. That was Bill.

The following events leading up to his death are sometimes overwhelming and can no longer be fathomed in any detail, including the chronological sequence. Especially because Bill and Anna Margarete didn't communicate with the family about many things. In any case, at the beginning of the 1990s both decided to leave their paradise in Powell River again. Perhaps it was due to age, as they could not count on quick help in the event of a medical emergency, and William was getting older. Maybe the daily work there just became too much for Anna Margarete, or was it just too lonely for her in the end? In any case, they sold everything and initially moved to a place called Nanaimo.[52] Margarete's daughter Christine lived there with her husband Bert. Initially they both moved into a townhouse on Stewart Avenue, a spacious house, but a studio still had to be built. William didn't like the house because the view was simply sobering for the nature lover. Only from a single window could you see a little bit of water in the distance. And so the two of them moved out again very quickly. This time it took them near Hammond Bay Road. The view there was a little better, the lake view now stretched across two windows, but here too a studio had to be set up first. And what William was missing in any case was a garden. Anna Margarete, on the other hand, felt very comfortable there. She enjoyed city life and was often with her daughter. But Bill kept trudging around the house, unfulfilled and grumbling. There was simply nothing for him to do here. He no longer had a workshop and nothing needed to be repaired here. There were neither creative projects nor even the smallest amount of gardening here. He didn't even have a boat anymore, and fishing was out of the question here anyway. So he always lost the desire to paint. As a result, he was then deeply frustrated and unbalanced; one can imagine that the previous slight cracks in their relationship were now deepening. In his last TV appearances, which was in 1992, he was noticeably different. As usual, he painted at his easel, but the fiery, the energy that he always radiated before was missing. His expression was petrified and the corners of his mouth pointed stubbornly downwards. Although he chatted as always, everything has become more leisurely and quieter. He repeatedly started sentences and then ended them abruptly. It seemed as if he had forgotten what he actually wanted to say. Only now and then did a spark of energy come through in him, making him smile briefly and reminding him of the good old TV days with Bill. His foster son naturally noticed a change in „Pop's" behaviour. And after working as a banker for many years, he took a break and has now established himself as a real estate agent. So one day he made a suggestion to Bill. Real estate prices were quite cheap at the time, and there was a nice house for sale right on the lake. He could have a boat there again and also go fishing. So they moved again. It was fine for a while, but the restlessness remained within him and only changed after he made a new decision. About 20 kilometers from Port Alberni, William bought a 20-acre farm. Here he would want to blossom again and create a paradise. But everything turned out completely differently.

The last big projects, and Bill's worst mistake

Bill's thirst for action came back again on the newly acquired farm, and all sorts of large projects flashed through his mind. A small river flowed through his land, and there was already a small fish pond on the huge property. Surely something could be made of this, he thought. But first he tore down the old barn and a new studio was to be built. Then finally he dedicated himself to the small river with the greatest enthusiasm and developed another of his expensive ideas, which was doomed to failure in the end, and made us outsiders of the whole event smile a little bit, and Bill became even more lovable for us, he becomes more humanly understandable. It occurred to him that the river could simply be diverted and a large trout pond would then be created near it. So Bill hired a guy to do the digging with heavy equipment. However, Bill forgot that such a river diversion was not allowed to be carried out without official approval. But he never actually thought about such things. Not out of malice or anything, but rather out of a certain childish naivety. And the guy with the heavy equipment didn't care anyway. He would get his money either way. So he enlarged the small pond, the hole was an impressive six meters deep at the end, and the diameter of the pond was just as respectable. A return to the river was then dug at one end, a connection was then made from the newly created pond to the previous course of the river, and the water was diverted to the new trout pond with a ceremonial ceremony and many a beer. At first everything looked very good and Bill put countless trout into the pond. So that they didn't simply swim away, he set up nets at the entrance and exit. Unfortunately, there was just something he hadn't considered. The river flow came to him from a neighboring property on higher ground, and this neighbor had a thriving pastoral economy. His herd of cattle was impressively large, and the faeces of these animals had been seeping from the pasture for ages straight into the small, slow-flowing river. Until now it had simply been washed away, but now it all flowed into William's pond and was gradually deposited there. The trout pond was also in the middle of the property, completely without bushes or trees that could have provided shade. A large electric pump was initially intended to prevent the worst and pump the accumulated feces from the pond back into the river. But that wasn't enough, and so the pond heated up more and more. Then in the summer, the trout pond had already mutated into a foul-smelling cloaca, all the fish swam only with their bellies upwards. If only he had removed the nets, the fish would at least have been able to save themselves. Resigned, he officially declared his pond project a failure. It was probably again around 10,000 dollars or even significantly more that he wasted, and here too he said with a mild smile: "Look, I have shown you once again how not to do it." Anna Margarete just rolled her eyes and shook her head.

But then something happened that he never forgave himself after. Nobody expected what was to happen next. Least of all probably Bill. He had always been a charmer in his public appearances and regularly flirted with his female fans. Everyone knew that, and his partner had no problem with it either, it was part of the deal. William was equally charming to each of his female fans. To the daughter as well as to the mother or her grandmother. It was just in his nature. It should be noted that he never allowed himself to be carried away into anything. He was charming, but he was also always respectful and never started anything with any of his admirers. He could have, because his female fans were sometimes very stubborn and knew exactly what they wanted. Many a love letter to him spoke clearly. One day, when he was in the middle of his big farm project, a young and dapper woman appeared in his life. But since Bill and Margarete never spoke in detail about the following, unfortunately all we know is that it was probably someone from his professional environment. It was about business and, at least this is still known, she skillfully used her feminine charms. How much genuine affection for Bill as a person, how much calculated business acumen lay behind it, no one knows, but one can guess. There is a small photograph of both of them. On the one hand, you see her there, the young beauty, slim and extremely elegant. She appears flirtatious and confident in the snapshot. Very confident. Next to it you can see William. He looks like an aging, comfortable and good-natured elephant next to her. . At first he resisted her advances, but at some point the old man gave in and let everything happen. This affair was quickly discovered; it is said that Anna Margarete even accidentally caught the two of them inflagrantially. At that moment the new paradise shattered! It was his last paradise, and there would be nothing new. The result was that Margarete immediately ended her relationship with William and moved out immediately. She moved into a small house in Port Alberni, while Bill remained alone out on the large farm. What happened is all the more dramatic when you think of Williams' words from 1983, with which he once described his partner Anna Margarete. He said about her: "Anna Margarete is a good friend, a real pearl and a good comrade. She is not just my wife, she is much more. She can do everything I can't. She has brains, she can read and write (in English), which I can't do perfectly. And she is the most honest woman in the world, she would never cheat on anyone!" It must have been incredibly painful for him to have hurt such a genuinely honest and pure person in this way. He worried about this until his death. Just a moment of weakness and he called it the biggest mistake of his life, something he never forgave himself for. The exact year cannot be determined precisely, but it is obvious that this all happened around the time when he disappeared from the

TV stage, i.e. around 1992. More dramas were already on the horizon and were inexorably making their way. Bill had always been a sociable guy and needed people around him. He liked being the center of attention and wanted to be perceived as a nice guy. But now he was all alone on his big farm. Resignation, loneliness and poor health all had a stronger effect on him than ever, but he was always too proud to ever talk about it. Who else could he have done it with? Anna Margarete had left and blocked all contact, his daughter Heidi had her own life, and friends in the new environment were also rare. Christine, Anna Margarete's daughter, lived too far away to come, and contact with William wasn't quite as close. Only his foster son stayed by his side and visited him regularly. He now let all the big plans for his farm slide, disinterested. The halfdemolished barn remained standing like a memorial, only the studio was still completed. William became more and more lethargic, there wasn't much left of the former „Happy Painter." In addition, he paid less and less attention to his health, no longer ate properly, and he categorically ignored taking all the necessary tablets anyway. At some point then he suffered his first stroke. Luckily he wasn't that strong and William was able to regenerate to some extent over time. A direct result of the stroke, however, was that he was no longer able to paint and act as energetically and energetically as before, but it still worked somehow, true to his motto: "Good enough is enough."

Thinking outside the box – Bill's "master series"

During this time Bill thought about a lot of things. About life, about death. But especially about his own role as an artist. Was he a good artist himself? Would he even be remembered in the future? To him, the "Happy Painter," the goodhumoured TV painter? Bill thought several times about the unpleasant moment when a guy watched him paint in public and said he was painting like Bob Ross. Of course, he noticed that his former student achieved worldwide fame with his painting technique, with the ingenious "Alexander painting technique" that he had developed. This invention was his life. But who would still think of him? What artistic legacy would he leave behind? Was there even one? He painted the same mountain with the lake in front of it dozens of times. Even if he let this landscape shine in a completely new light each time - Monet himself created such series pictures - was it enough in the end to remember him? He probably feared that it wouldn't be so. When his foster son came to visit and reprimanded him again for not taking all his medications conscientiously enough, they would always talk about this topic for a long time. At one point, Bill asked him directly how the world would remember him. His foster son thought for a while and said: "You were the lucky TV painter who delivered a safe and uncontroversial product. Precisely to the minute. You taught the world to paint in oils and you invented the ingenious "Magic White" - and the diamond-shaped palette knife too. But it's unlikely that you'll be remembered as a great artist. In short, your pictures don't move people much emotionally or intellectually. They are just pretty and for a long time people wanted to have pictures like that. But today people like different pictures, and your pictures are paintings that your own students could easily reproduce at any time. Are these really masterpieces in the end?" These words may sound brutal to us, but his foster son did not choose these words without consideration. Bill had already thought extensively about the topic of "masterpieces" and "master series" in the mid-1980s.[53] Masterpieces, these were pictures outside the norm. Something special and great, and not every artist will be able to paint one. He repeatedly asked himself whether he would ever be able to be remembered as a "master." He didn't make it to this conversation yet. When Bill heard his words, he breathed heavily, and after a while he nodded almost imperceptibly. He seemed far away at that moment. He kept rocking his head back and forth and humming something quietly. After a while, his foster son asked why he had never been a "true artist" who made statements with his pictures. Why only landscapes and still lifes? He could have been much more diverse in his choice of subjects. Also in terms of content. He said: "Pop, you've talked so often about war and power, about greed and money and the resulting catastrophes for people. Likewise about the institution of the church, which rules over people. Why have you never taken up these topics and processed them artistically? Pop, why did you paint almost the same pictures over and over again? Because you never thought outside the box, this omission could actually have a limiting effect on how you are viewed as an artist after your death." Of course, Bill didn't like hearing that at all and replied forcefully that, first of all, it was his The first priority is to give his audience what they expect. In addition, many people around him make a living through his work. It should not be forgotten that Bill also had a large number of students who became teachers themselves and many more who wanted to become teachers. He couldn't stop everything because he saw a responsibility towards his students. Finally, he added that he was very happy with what he was doing, namely making others happy and making a living doing what he was very happy with himself. Bill said nothing more for a while and seemed to think again about everything he had said. Then he looked at his foster son and said much more quietly: „As much as I want to paint what I see on the dark side, I can't make anything good of it right now. But if I do, you'll be the first, Sandy." Secretly, of course, Bill knew that his foster son was right. For decades he preached again and again that his students "should be almighty creators on the screen." But he himself reduced himself to what he always did. It was long overdue that he too had to think outside the box again.

A few months passed during which Talore checked in on Bill regularly, just as children do with their aging parents. They didn't say a single word about their recent conversation, and fortunately Bill's health had stabilized to some extent. But they did talk again and again about great and important artists in general, or about those they didn't really like. Well, at least William did that. His foster son was a banker and broker, and he was never really into art. There were a few pictures of William hanging in his room, but that was enough for him. But when he came up with a name that he really liked, Bill sometimes turned up his nose and pretended he hadn't heard it. Picasso[54] was one of those candidates that he didn't like at all. In general, modern art[55] was not at all to his taste. When he saw a painting in a gallery that only had a blob on it, he always asked what he was actually seeing there. Is it a tree? Or a shoe? Maybe a bear? When he was in the mood, he would like to go a little further with a grin: "If I'm out and about all day, working and having to make decisions and solve problems, then I don't want to sit at home in the evening in front of a picture and keep thinking about it I have to ask myself what I'm actually seeing. I don't even know whether it's something happy that's depicted there or is it something sad?" No, he was fundamentally at odds with modern art. Customers repeatedly asked him if he would paint something modern for them. William always categorically refused.

With a smile, he then told the story of the TV show he once saw. The presenter presented a modern picture on an easel. There were lines and little blobs on it. He asked a lady if she could recognize what the picture showed and asked if she could see that it depicted a sea. The lady confirmed it. And whether she would also recognize the small boats. The lady nodded then too. Then the presenter grinned smugly at her and said: "Oh, sorry, my mistake. The picture is upside down on the easel." After turning it over, he asked again whether the lady could see the sea and the boats. William then waved it off and said that people would just see what they were told to see in the picture. One painter he absolutely admired, however, was the American Charles M. Russell.[56)] He lived in the 19th century and was a painter, sculptor, graphic artist, writer and even a real cowboy. Russell painted impressive paintings depicting the people and nature of North America. He created countless pictures about the lives of the settlers and native people and showed how they went about their everyday lives, drove cattle or hunted. His paintings were a firework of colors, light and shadows. And they were so incredibly detailed. William loved these paintings. In every bar across Montana, Bill once wrote with amusement, there is at least one picture of Charles M. Russell, who used to trade his paintings for a few beers in the saloon. "My goodness," Bill mused, "Russell must have drunk a lot of beer in his life."

In the months that followed, he heard very little of Pop. Most of the time he didn't have time and only spoke briefly on the phone. "He had work to do," they always said. The young father of the family was basically happy, as he already had enough to do in his own life. One day, however, Bill called him completely excited and he literally shouted into the phone that he had to come immediately. On the spot! He left everything behind, because when Pop called so unexpectedly, then something really bad must have happened. 20 minutes and a red traffic light later, he reached the farm. Bill literally dragged him out of the car and literally pushed him straight into his studio: "Look, Sandy, what I have secretly created in the last few months." Bill was excited and proud at the same time. He was shaking with joy inside and it seemed as if he had all his lost strength back. He was as excited as a little boy. Four large screens stood next to each other in front of the two men. Two paintings had already been completed, two were still in progress. These pictures were so different from anything Bill had ever painted. Across North America and Canada, pictures of William hung on walls or lay asleep in attics. But no one had ever seen anything like this from William. Both agreed on that. These were not beautiful landscapes, this was something completely new! Something special. But also something frightening! In fact, Bill had in the last few months set out to paint what he saw on the dark side. He pulled his foster son aside and told him that he was the only one who knew about these paintings so far. And despite his illness, the aging William Alexander had actually managed to think outside the box artistically. He always wanted people to grow beyond themselves and dare to try new things. Now he too had finally left the safe haven of his profession. He encountered new territory in which he had to find his way and express himself in a new way. He addressed complex themes in his pictures and looked for symbolic forms of expression, which he found. If only he had done this sooner and more consistently, the world would probably remember him differently today. Pop and Sandy watched the series for a long time, and Sandy was proud. On the one hand, on what Pop had created, but also a little bit on himself, because it was he who motivated him to do this. And William was proud too. He had successfully managed to reach new shores. He had proven it to himself and Sandy, and that made him happy inside. But both of them also completely agreed that these were not pictures that Bill's typical customer would want to hang in their living room. Little by little, William showed his immediate surroundings, colleagues and friends, his new series. The reactions to this were mixed. At the time of its creation, most people found it unsympathetic. They didn't answer or reacted evasively. Some found them extremely expressive, but only a few. The discouragement was great and many strongly advised him not to exhibit them publicly. The reason for this may, however, be that these dissuading people made a living from selling his usual art or the courses offered. Who could have known what effect such a realignment would have? They were never publicly exhibited during his lifetime. That was fine with him too, he had proven what he could do. But he said to his foster son: "If you ever publish these images, make sure they are presented in the light in which they are intended. This means that war is hell, especially for those directly exposed to it. But it's not a walk in the park for the families who are only indirectly affected." Bill loved the peace and tranquility of nature. But the reality of humanity at its worst was never lost on him. So if Bill wanted to stand out from the crowd, I'd like to say he did a pretty good job of letting the world know that he could be a serious artist. But in the end he just decided he didn't want to be! The deterioration of William's health and his death are the reason that two of the paintings remained unfinished. I recently showed the photos from the "Master Series" to a well-known curator at a large gallery. At first I was amazed that the curator even knew William Alexander, which of course made me very happy. In addition, he was also amazed that William painted political allegories[57] and that he was able to express himself in such symbolic complexity. The pictures are still in the family's possession to this day.

The imagery of his completed pictures is definitely reminiscent of the imagery critical of capitalism from the 1920s to 1930s. Well-known names also come to mind such as George Grosz,[58] the early Emil Nolde with his mountain faces,[59] Siqueros[60] and Orozco,[61] as well as the Mexican painter Rivera.[62] The first painting (photo below) primarily denounces the war. In the foreground of the red, yellow and violet picture is the blood-red river, on whose banks there are contorted corpses and dying people. People and animal, l, they all die, and the blood from their bodies escapes into the river. A tank is preparing to overrun people and animals. In the foreground on the right, directly on the bank, there are two clergymen of different faiths. Their headgear glows, as if they themselves were illuminated, which is something leaders of religious communities like to use to control their followers. The two calmly wash their hands in the blood of the river. William repeatedly expressed himself extremely critically in his TV show, but also in his autobiography, with regard to the role of the church and other religious organizations. He was of the opinion

Completed and signed painting from the "Master Series" by William "Bill" Alexander
Photo: Private collection

that no one should make themselves small before God, and that God didn't want that. Man stands right next to God, as he put it. And one should certainly not make oneself small in front of the church leaders. He repeatedly specifically named several religious leaders in this context.[63] What is also striking in the painting is that a head can be seen far in the background, between the clouds. The iconography seems clear. This head represents the capitalist with a big cigar and dollar signs on his sunglasses. He is cold, callous and power conscious. Capitalism and war are closely intertwined. In the past as well as today. Centrally above all the suffering, the fighting and the dying, a being made of fire flies over the scenario. It appears to be horned, or is it just random flames shooting up from the creature? In any case, it laughs and is probably happy about the reaper's bountiful harvest. Opposite, directly in the rock massif, the viewer discovers another head. He appears as part of nature, crying, helplessly enduring the situation, he probably represents the emphatic person who wants to live in peace. Self-responsible, and not serving - or being used - as a helpless plaything of the powerful.

The second painting, in the same format, (photo below) obviously focuses on the capitalist war profiteer to whose tune the world must dance. Fat, unyielding and clutching the world, this is how the artist depicts him here. There is no doubt who has power on the planet. Money is already piling up in his hand, blood money certainly, but on the North American continent there are rockets. To the left behind the capitalist, surrounded by powerful cannon barrels, projectiles and all sorts of satellite dishes, is an archaic-looking warrior on horseback.

The second completed and signed painting from William „Bill" Alexander's „Master Series."

Photo: Private collection

Rearing up, wearing a headdress with horns, armed only with a simple saber. He won't be able to do much there. On the right, also pushed into the background, a head of a native of this continent looking out of the clouds. He appears peaceful and friendly, completely at peace with himself. But he also looks worried and composed towards the viewer. This head appears to be a counterpart to the mountain head in the previous image. But in this arrangement he also seems almost like a trophy, like one of those shrunken heads that the winner created by the defeated enemy in order to then wear it on a ribbon from then on. But these are all just the perspectives of one individual. Maybe William wants to tell us something completely different. These images have not yet been analyzed in terms of content, and William has not left anything behind regarding their interpretation and analysis, so that we all have the exciting opportunity to approach these images and their symbolic code individually. Let us now dedicate ourselves to the two remaining paintings. Prevented illness and deathits completion, so that much will remain in the dark. But we also discover some symbolism in them that we already discovered in the completed paintings.

The central figure in this picture (photo right) is a helpless man tied to a chair with his skull open. Behind him, in the center and surrounded by a halo of light that may resemble an aureole, stands a religious dignitary. His headgear makes it easy to identify him as a religion. With both hands he reaches into the defenseless man's skull, whose face is distorted with extreme pain and despair is. He kicks his legs wildly, but there is no release for him.

One of the two unfinished paintings from the "Master Series" by William "Bill" Alexander. Photo: Private collection

Two helpers, whose hoods are reminiscent of the robes of monks, support this clergyman. Vast quantities of liquid drip from the opened skull onto the blood-red floor. What does it represent? Does it symbolize "brainwashing?" The helper on the left is holding something in his hand, but it cannot be clearly assigned because it is still unfinished. Possibly it is a vessel with smoking incense that is held under the man's nose. One could superficially interpret the symbolism to mean that clergy are fighting for the salvation of an unbeliever and carrying out an exorcism in order to free him from false faith. But since we are now quite familiar with the artist's views, the scene certainly represents something completely different. Here we see how religious dignitaries implant something into a person's brain that they do not want to have. There is brainwashing going on here. This person may represent humanity in general, into which fear and superstition are being instilled so that they accept a higher power and its elite and submit to them. Because, as we know, nothing makes you as pious as fear.

Even in this unfinished painting (photo below) the topic of religion, self-determination and external determination is discussed again. In the foreground on the left is the group of those who act self-determined. Free from superstition and foreign dominance. They sit enthroned on a naturalistically painted mountain range. The landscape behind them shows

The second unfinished painting from the William "Bill" Alexander's "Master Series."

forests and a river disappearing into the background, creating a strong spatial depth. The left background area is in green tones - but is still unfinished. Among them The fog billows up, which further elevates this group on the mountain top. A person equipped with a spear, who radiates both strength and wisdom, points with an outstretched arm to the group shown on the right, which is clearly shown below them. The entire right area is dominated by blazing red, yellow and purple hues. A group of people crouch on the floor at the bottom right, above them stands a frightening fiery figure, reminiscent of the flying creature in the first painting. This horned creature also involuntarily reminds us of the hellish figures painted in the 13th century by the Florentine painter Buonamico Buffalmacco.[64] There is blaze and smoke everywhere. This fire creature seems to be trying to scare the group on the mountain as well. And while the left side of the picture appears to the viewer as harmonious and peaceful, the right area can be classified as frightening. In the middle, between these two very different groups, there is a cloud. There is a group of religious dignitaries on it. Here too we discover old acquaintances from the first painting. The two dignitaries who washed their hands in the river of blood there also sit together centrally, being courted by those around them. The religious groups can be easily assigned based on the headgear. The clergy look up at the group on the left, spellbound. It seems as if they wanted to see whether the fire creature, this personification of fear and superstition, could harm the group. Behind the cloud with the clergy, at the very top of the picture, a head appears again, blending harmoniously with the mountains. This head towers over all groups. But what does it stand for? Unlike the weeping head, this one appears sublime and knowing, giving strength. Is it perhaps the personification of nature? Or is it a symbol of the human mind that sees through superstition?

The last years

Then one day William suffered a second stroke. Much worse than the first time. So bad that he could no longer live on the farm alone. From then on, William needed comprehensive care. He was no longer even able to continue painting, let alone handle everyday life on his own. Talore recalled that he never saw Pop as insecure in his life as he was at that time. A solution had to be found, and so his foster son campaigned for a reconciliation with Anna Margarete. The farm was quickly sold and a free house was purchased in Port Alberni. The first thing Bill did was build a studio next to the house. However, his efforts to paint again and achieve any desired result proved unsuccessful. Ultimately, Bill couldn't or didn't want to paint in this house anymore, and he couldn't or didn't want to do anything to improve the property, which he and Anna Margarete always did. It seemed as if he had lost all interest in life and he would just sit and look at the sky or the garden. But there wasn't much to see in this house, so they decided to move again. The last one in his life. A good four kilometers from his foster son's house, they found a suitable place to live on 2nd Avenue. It was nothing compared to the houses and land Bill once owned. It was the last house on a small street with typical suburban houses. There they stood, made of wood. Small rectangular one-story houses, many of which looked pretty much the same. Nothing spectacular. This house stood directly on a small intersection, Striling Street, which sloped westwards at a noticeable gradient. Directly down to the harbor of Port Alberni. Since the house was built on a slope, there was only one level on the street side. On the opposite side, facing west, there was another floor below this level. The house was surrounded on three sides by a very small strip of green on which a few dry bushes were vegetating. But the view was very beautiful, the water was less than 200 meters away and behind it a gentle mountain range. The house was registered in Anna Margarete's name and William had a lifelong right of residence. She looked after him and cared for him, they both lived under the same roof, but they still remained separated. I would like to address one aspect at this point. We heard about the many moves, William repeatedly bought land and houses, he invested in the properties and improved the facilities, thus increasing their sales value. That definitely had method. He knew nothing about financial transactions, but he knew from his East Prussian youth that owning land, land and houses, was something good and profitable. The blue bloods had shown him that back then. So when he had money available, he preferred to buy properties. And he was skilled at it. For example, many years ago, he once bought a hectare of land in Langley, BC. There was even a wooden house on it, at the time only inhabited by countless termites. But it only cost $10,000 at the time, so he bought it. They also lived there for a time, and at night you could always hear the termites hard at work. None of this bothered him because he saw that the property had potential. When Bill's foster son came to visit, he motivated him to paint another picture. The way Bill taught him, or at least tried to. However, the painting he created only caused people to shake their heads and Bill said that it was all just mud on the canvas. "Come with me, Sandy," he said, "I have a better job for you." Then he gave the boy paints, a ladder and brushes so that he could paint the front of the house instead. The boy was definitely more clever at this. Bill would pay him a few dollars for his work and left the boy alone. When he came back, he was amazed and laughed. Sandy had learned from Bill. So that he could earn his money more quickly, the boy stood on the ladder and simply painted with both hands. And, yes, it looked very good. William later came up with the idea of painting the entire facade of the house with a landscape, and from then on there were always traffic jams on the street in front of his house because drivers stopped and took photos of it. Well, this property is now estimated to be worth a million dollars. And even then, when William sold it again, he made a good living with it.

And even now, after his second stroke, he at least still had the joy of investing. One day he learned from the newspaper that cheap properties were being offered in the province of Saskatchewan, in a town called Naicam.[65] A recession hit this town particularly hard. You have to know that this province was at least 2000 kilometers away from Bill's house and he couldn't even take care of himself. But Bill wanted it. Absolutely! He wanted to go to Naicam to buy property there. And immediately. One might of course suspect a certain rigidity of age at this point. Anna Margarete immediately dismissed this. Such a strain? Not with her. So there was only one left. Talore. Of course he was "extremely happy" when he heard about the new, crazy idea. Because Talore had completely different things going on at the moment, he recently became a father again and he had also started a new job. But since no one else was available, he agreed. For the next two weeks he was Bill's driver, his 24-hour carer, personally financial advisor and general supervisor. Bill really blossomed at that time and decided on a five-hectare property with countless outbuildings. The purchase price was just $17,500. The land had good black soil, which was ideal for rich yields. Bill was very familiar with it. This house could be a very nice retreat if you like annoying flies in summer and freezing cold in winter. Of course, he no longer used it so really. This trip was his last big adventure because his health no longer improved, on the contrary, he physically deteriorated. William preferred to spend the last few days before his death sitting on a bench in front of his small house. From there he looked on the water from morning to evening. Port Alberni has a busy harbor and there was always a lot of activity on the water. He enjoyed it, there was always something to see there. Small and large ships, many people who were busy loading and then the many small sailing boats that cruised around sportily. In the evening the sun sank behind the rolling mountain range, creating a light that Bill captured in his paintings for decades.

He sat down at the easel once more and wanted to create one more of his beloved landscapes. Large trees tower in the background of the landscape format image. Firs and deciduous trees. In the foreground there is a calm body of water, flanked on the left and right by bushes and trees. A small bridge in the middle of the picture leads from left to right. Maybe he remembered the encounter at the Eastern Front when he met the Russian soldier on

A small and spontaneously made thumbnail sketch by me, with the view from William's house in Port Alberni down to the harbor and the mountains - as well as a side view (JM Müller, November 2023)

the bridge? On the water (photo on the next page), in the foreground of the picture, you can see countless white-yellowish water lilies. Bill's motor skills were far too limited to paint a really good picture. In terms of craftsmanship, this painting is clearly behind what he was previously able to conjure up on canvas. And instead of his previous massive signature, there is only on the bottom right edge small, faintly applied initials.

On the evening of January 24, 1997, Bill was not feeling well and went to bed early. Later that evening, Anna Margarete heard strange noises coming from his room and called her son, who immediately got into the car. After a few minutes he arrived and rushed straight into the bedroom. He found William lying in bed motionless and without a pulse and immediately called an ambulance. The paramedics tried to resuscitate him and took him to the West Coast General Hospital, just four kilometers away, but all they could determine there was that he was dead. William Aexander died of a heart attack. The cremation took place on January 28th. The subsequent funeral service was held in the "Chapel of Memories" in Port Alberni. At the end of the long and decorated chapel, with its pointed wooden roof, a lectern and the urn were placed. A straight path led from the entrance to the chapel to the lectern, flanked on the left and right by rows of wooden benches. About thirty mourners gathered that day. Including William's daughter Heidi with his 13-year-old granddaughter Heather. At that time, Heidi was already separated from her husband and had to fend for herself. Anna Margarete was of course also present, as was her daughter Christine. William's foster son appeared with his wife and children.

The last painted by William "Bill" Alexander Landscape before his death. Photo: Private collection

Some friends from the town also said goodbye, as did Don Gerdts, who had come specially for this event from Los Angeles. Talore gave the eulogy, and as he wrote it beforehand, he recalled, he cried like a little child. Because you often only realize the magnitude of a loss when you experience it. In his speech he spoke of what was important to William. The nature, the fishing, he probably also told some stories about it and spoke of what Bill called "a better tomorrow." Bill's wish was that his ashes would be spread in the sea; he wanted to be with his beloved fish. So after the funeral service, a small convoy set off towards Nanaimo. On the approximately 80 kilometer long journey there, they also passed Cameron Lake. Bill came here repeatedly to fish. There were sockeye salmon in abundance, as well as Pacific salmon, rainbow trout and much more. The area was also picturesque and is still a very popular tourist region today. From Nainamo they went directly to the boat harbor via Cedar. There was already a boat waiting for the mourning community. It was a former missionary ship, around 17 meters long, that used to sail up and down the coast and was intended to spread the faith. Later, Talore's stepsister's husband bought it. After the lines were released, they headed north past Flewett Point, a peninsula, directly into the „Strait of Georgia." There, between the east coast of Vancouver Island and the coast of British Columbia, lie the idyllic „Gulf Islands." The first small islands, which have such exotic names as „Mudge Island," „Ruxton Island" or „De Courcy Island," on which the beautiful „Pirates Cove Marine Provincial Park" can be found, are just around 4 kilometers from Cedars boat harbor. The whole area is picturesque, and many of the islands are part of a large nature reserve with lush forests and picturesque coastlines. And if you're a little lucky, you can see the orcas playing in the sea. The funeral party's destination was in the middle of the „GuldIslands," less than two kilometers from the port (the coordinates are approximately (DG) 49.116556, -123.786077). Towards the north, northeast you could see the tapering sound that leads directly to the „Dodd Narrows," the attraction that forms a bottleneck between Vancouver Island and „Mudge Island." The water there flows quickly and is in some areas crystal clear. A picturesque spot that Bill loved. Here, in this idyllic setting, here they gave his ashes to the sea. After the small ceremony, we had a small snack on board and toasted Bill. Since then, Anna Margarete has lived in seclusion in her house in Port Alberni; she no longer maintained any major contacts, and she also had a falling out with her daughter. Only her son visited her every now and then and they drank coffee and he reported news about his life, or they just played cards. Just a few years ago she died in a retirement home, probably of lung cancer, because she smoked a lot throughout her life. She too was cremated and her ashes were then thrown into the sea at the exact spot where Bill had been waiting for her since 1997. Off a picturesque coast off Vancouver Island, directly in the „Strait of Georgia," both are now forever united after their deaths.

What else is there to report? Not much anymore. Bill died neither a rich man nor a poor man. The executor took care of the sale of the existing ones property. For example, the property in the town of Naicam, which was recently purchased in the province of Saskatchewan, only achieved a sales price of $10,000 because everything had to happen quikkly (at that time, Naicam was at the end of the world, today it is a very sought-after address with corresponding property prices). In order to avoid possible inheritance disputes in advance, a lawyer was commissioned to carry out the distribution. At that time, daughter Heidi received 80 percent of the inheritance, the rest was distributed among Anna Margarete and her children. Talore received, among other things, Bill's last paintings, as well as countless brushes, painting knives and paint tubes that could probably still be used today. He was the only one who was even interested in his last paintings. The executor of the estate still reported, but we can't research all of this in more detail, so I just want to mention it without comment for the sake of order that Sid Knudsen sold his company for around 1 million dollars after Bill's death. At the time, this company probably made around $3 million in sales per year. However, the buyer, a certain Mr. Schneider, died in a tragic accident. The next buyer was still known by name, but nothing more precise can be reported. According to the executor, William Alexander's family did not receive any royalties from the company's new owner, even though the company still advertised with his name. It's not that easy to say whether there is a claim at all; since the family didn't have enough capital, they were never able to hire a lawyer.

This spot is William „Bill" Alexander's final resting place

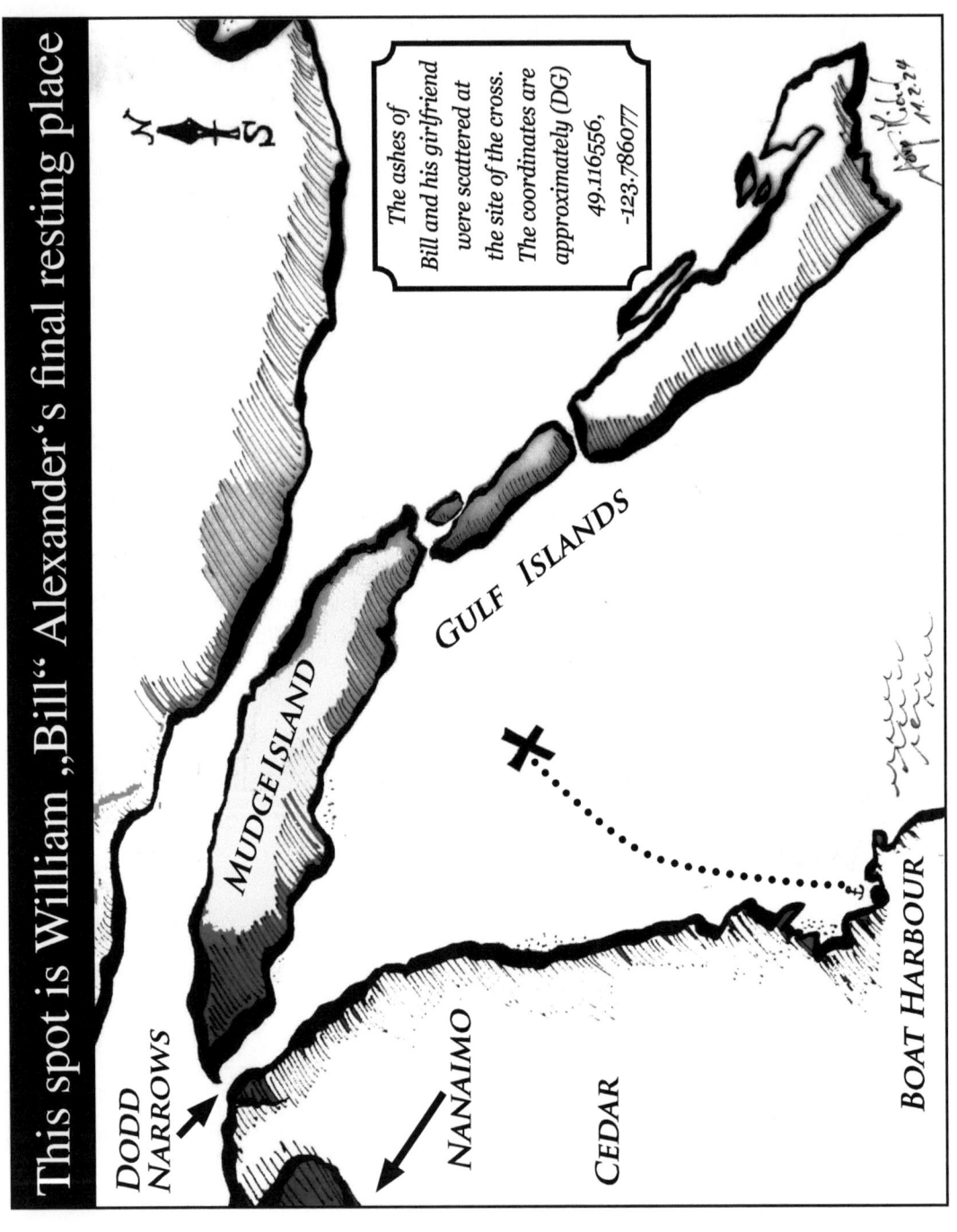

The ashes of Bill and his girlfriend were scattered at the site of the cross. The coordinates are approximately (DG) 49.116556, -123.786077

DODD NARROWS

MUDGE ISLAND

GULF ISLANDS

NANAIMO

CEDAR

BOAT HARBOUR

Epilogue

We accompanied William Alexander on his long and exciting journey through life, and we were able to fear, hope, laugh and even cry with him. Bill was a do-gooder, a dreamer and a romantic for whom the glass was always half full, even on bad days. He longed for an ideal world. He, who experienced the horrors of war in the trenches and was wounded several times, dreamed of a better tomorrow, of a better future. For yourself, for you, for everyone on this planet. He wished that all people could lead happy and self-determined lives. In peace and in harmony with nature. He rejected any form of oppression, whether by self-proclaimed elites or religious leaders. For him, all people were equal.

And what modern thoughts William Alexander had. At a time when mineral oil companies were still carelessly polluting entire areas of land in order to maximize profits, he was already thinking about complex species protection and the preservation of biodiversity and developed fish breeding and bird protection programs. At a time when the Cold War was still in its heated phase, he regularly spoke out on his TV show against the scourge of humanity, man-made war. He repeatedly emphasized the horrors that war entails, which he had to experience first hand. And many a time he abruptly interrupted himself so as not to slip deeper into the horror reports, he almost implored that something like that shouldn't happen again, that people should learn from what had happened. And how little we humans have developed in our societies around the globe. Almost 80 years after the Second World War, one would think that in civilized countries the understanding should have become established that they never want to wage wars again.

And how little of it is implemented in the end. Even today, just in time for every new war, as current news in Ukraine teaches us, it is primarily the arms companies that rejoice and whose shares promise huge price gains. Let's take the German Rheinmetall share as an example. The company supplies, among other things, tanks and large quantities of ammunition. Before the invasion of Russian troops, the share was still at 96.44 euros on February 18, 2022. As early as March 4, 2022, it shot up to 148.70 euros. Today, December 20, 2023, there it is on one Record high of over 282 euros. Of course, this could also be a coincidence. But doesn't the painting with the globe from Bill's „Master Series" inevitably come to mind? For the sake of completeness, it should be noted that US defense stocks, such as those from

Boeing, Northrop Grumman, Lockheed Martin, General Dynamics and Raytheon, also rose noticeably in the same period. But we don't want to go into this any further here.

Let's think about something positive now, why not about a better future? William always encouraged his audience to try everything to live a happy life. Live by your convictions and act accordingly. Don't waste your life being an insignificant cog in someone else's machine. Do what makes you happy. Privately, and also at work... Especially at work. So let's risk being happy. German comedian Karl Valentin once said: "I'm happy when it rains. Because if I'm not happy, it'll rain too." A nice sentence that our friend Bill would definitely have signed. So let's look forward to whatever else we can do to fill the canvas of our lives. And if you ever see someone painting "Magic White" on a canvas, think of our friend Bill. Or better yet, be the one to apply the paint yourself. Become an almighty creator in front of your canvas. Right know would be good. So, dear reader: "Fire in!"

Sources and explanations:

1) William Alexander's autobiography was published in 1983. "The Bill Alexander Story: An Autobiography." ISBN:0-8403-2990-3. p.234.

2) KOCE-TV produced a 45-minute documentary about William Alexander in 1983, which can be seen on
YouTube: https://www.youtube.com/watch?v=OKEPISA0f4E
(accessed December 18, 2023).

3) „The Bill Alexander Story: An Autobiography." ISBN:0-8403-2990-3.

4) Some episodes of the TV series "The Magic of Oil Painting" are listed on YouTube: https://www.youtube.com/watch?v=-iXM6yZfdbs&t=543s (accessed on December 18, 2023).

5) Powell River is a small town in British Columbia located at the end of Highway 101 on the west coast of Canada. The small town has been known for its paper production since 1912. Even though this small town is close to big cities, such as Vancouver, Powell River can only be reached by ferry or plane. The place was named after Israel Wood Powell, a well-known doctor, politician, entrepreneur and land speculator who lived from April 27, 1836 to February 25, 1915.

6) Port Alberni is a small town in the province of British Columbia and is located on Vancouver Island, on the west coast of Canada.

7) The Counts of Dohna are a widespread noble family that have been mentioned since 1156. Since 1500, one of the lines has also been based in East Prussia, from where they were expelled after the end of the Second World War. One of the personalities of the 20th century was Heinrich Graf zu Dohna-Schlobitten, a career officer in the First World War who was reactivated as a general staff officer in the Second World War. He left the Wehrmacht in 1943 at his own request. Since he maintained contacts with the conspirators of July 20th, he was executed in Plötzensee on September 14th, 1944 after the coup failed. Shortly before his execution he wrote to his wife: "This is my farewell letter. How incredibly difficult it is to say goodbye for life without seeing each other again, without a hug, without a last kiss! – But God arranged it that way, I follow Him. He guided me throughout this entire time. I haven't had a weak moment so far, hopefully I'll stay strong until the end. I have always felt your prayers, and especially yours. Now you too have to stay strong, despite all the pain. I always asked Christ to hold my hand during these difficult times. He did and kept me strong."

8) The Counts Finck von Finckenstein are an East Prussian noble family who first acquired a family seat there in 1474. They were among the large landowners country. The acquired land alone, which belonged to Schönberg Castle, extended over 9,000 hectares. It was owned by the family until 1945. After 1945 it was burned down by the Soviet troops and is still a ruin today... like many other properties of that time.

9) The Dönhoffs are an old Westphalian noble family that spread across the Baltics to Poland and Prussia. They had also been based in East Prussia since 1640, where they resided in Friedrichstein Castle until 1945. In 1945 the castle was set on fire and destroyed by the Red Army.

10) Rautenberg (Russian: Uslovoje) is located around 40 kilometers from the district town of Tilsit. The place name probably comes from Gottfried Rautenberg, who acquired the site there in 1772. The Rautenberg family emigrated to East Prussia from the Lower Saxony area between Hildesheim and Celle. The Rautenberg community was first mentioned in documents in 1818. In 2010 the community still had 562 residents.

11) An efficient method that was used in East Prussia was the laying of clay tubes fired directly in the region, which were buried to a depth of 40 centimeters and through which the moisture in the soil was specifically drained away.

12) The House of Hohenzollern was one of the most important dynasties in German history, named after its ancestral home, Hohenzollern Castle in Swabia.

13) The Battle of Tannenberg took place south of Allenstein in East Prussia from August 26th to August 30th, 1914 between German and Russian armies. The German troops, led by Hindenburg and Ludendorff, as well as Hoffmann and von François, were victorious, and the battle ended with the destruction of the Russian army that had invaded southern East Prussia.

14) The Winter Battle of Masuria took place from February 7th to February 22nd, 1915 between German and Russian troops. Even though it ended with a victory for the Germans, their goals of completely destroying the 10th Russian Army were not achieved because the remnants of the 10th Army were able to get to safety in time.

15) The Franco-Prussian War of 1870-1871 was a military conflict between France and the North German Confederation led by Prussia and their allies. The war was triggered by the dispute between France and Prussia over Prince Leopold of Hohenzollern-Sigmaringen's candidacy for the Spanish throne, which escalated because Bismarck sent a letter to the French court that was so intentionally provocative that Napoleon III. therefore felt compelled to declare war on Prussia on July 19, 1870. Bismark's calculations worked. However, the French troops could not hold their ground, France lost, and this war officially ended on May 10, 1871.

16) The Great Depression was triggered by the stock market crash in New York in October 1929. The most important consequences of the crisis were the massive decline in industrial production and world trade. There was inflation and banking crises, bankruptcies and continent-wide mass unemployment.

17) George Smith Patton Jr. (November 11, 1885 to December 21, 1945) was a US general in World War II. In addition to missions in North Africa and Sicily, he commanded the 3rd US Army on the Western Front after the Normandy landings. He died unexpectedly in a car accident and was buried in Luxembourg, with "his" men from the 3rd Army.

18) Research did not reveal a US prisoner of war camp with the number "401" near Marseille. Although there was a Camp 401 for German prisoners of war, it was located directly in the USA. However, there was a POW camp that would fit William's description. This is the camp CCPWE 404 (Continental Central Prisoner of War Enclosure number 404). It was located about 20 kilometers north of Marseille, near the town of Calas. its department stores are known across Canada under the Hudson's Bay brand.

19) For the city of Giessen, almost two thirds of the houses were destroyed, the Second World War ended on March 28, 1945 around 3 p.m. when the US soldiers invaded. After the end of the war, the city played a special role in the American occupation zone, as Giessen was to be expanded into the largest supply location in Europe.

20) Halifax (officially Halifax Regional Municipality, HRM) with over 400,000 inhabitants is the capital of the province of Nova Scotia in Canada. It is located on the North Atlantic east coast.

21) Nova Scotia is a Canadian province on the east coast, located on the North Atlantic.

22) Toronto, one of the country's most important metropolises, is the capital of the Canadian province of Ontario and lies on the northwest shore of Lake Ontario.

23) The Hudson's Bay Company (HBC, French Compagnie de la Baie d'Hudson) is a Canadian trading company founded in 1670. The Hudson's Bay Company is the oldest incorporated company in Canada. It controlled the fur trade for centuries until its decline in the 19th century. The company realigned itself into a trading company that sold vital goods to settlers in the Canadian West. Today society is for its department stores are known across Canada under the Hudson's Bay brand.

24) Densely populated Vancouver is a busy seaport on the west coast of British Columbia. 22) Toronto, one of the country's most important metropolises, is the capital of the Canadian province of Ontario and lies on the northwest shore of Lake Ontario. 21) Nova Scotia is a Canadian province on the east coast, located on the North Atlantic.

25) Montreal is the largest city in the Canadian province of Quebec and is located on a Island in the Saint Lawrence River.

26) Casa Loma (Spanish for "house on the hill") is a castle-like mansion in Toronto, Canada, which was built as a residential building by Sir Henry Pellatt from 1911 to 1914 for approximately 3.5 million Canadian dollars and is located at the north end of the in the Spadina Avenue on Davenport Hill.

27) The Hollywood Hills are a range of hills in the Hollywood District above the city of Los Angeles in the US state of California. They are the easternmost part of the Santa Monica Mountains and a popular residential area with mostly expensive villa developments.

28) The Greek district of Greektown, also known as "The Danforth", is known and popular for its international restaurants, cafes and bars, especially Greek taverns and patisseries.

29) Léry is a small town on the south shore of Lake Saint-Louis in Quebec, Canada. The town is located on Route 132, west of Châteauguay.

30) The Saint Lawrence River (French Fleuve Saint-Laurent; English Saint Lawrence River) is the third largest river in North America and flows into the Atlantic Ocean.

31) Aldergrove is a Canadian community in the township of Langley in British Columbia, located almost 60 kilometers east of Vancouver. This community is characterized by mainly agricultural use, including the cultivation of medical cannabis.

32) Artist George Rammell was born in Cranbrook, BC. He studied at the Vancouver School of Art and
has since worked as a sculptor and art teacher.

33) Anna Margarete sings and William plays the violin from minute 39 in the following documentary: https://www.youtube.com/watch?v=OKEPISA0f4E (accessed on December 18, 2023).

34) https://www.youtube.com/watch?v=ug5ywFeTSL4&t=987s (accessed on December 18, 2023).

35) „The Bill Alexander Story: An Autobiography." ISBN:0-8403-2990-3. S.94.

36) KOCE-TV (channel 50) is a PBS member television station licensed to Huntington Beach, California and serving the Los Angeles area.

37) Errol Leslie Thomson Flynn (June 20, 1909 – October 14, 1959) was an Australian-American film actor. He played the leading role in numerous classics from the 1930s to 1940s, such as „Under the Pirate Flag," „Robin Hood - King of the Vagabonds" or „The Lord of the Seven Seas." Towards the end of his career, his acting success waned, and the His time was marked by his alcoholism and financial problems.

38) John William "Johnny" Carson (October 23, 1925 - January 23, 2005) was an American show host and one of the best-known entertainers in the USA. From 1962 Until 1992 he was talk show host of "The Tonight Show," the most successful late-night show on American television.

39) Mikhail Sergeyevich Gorbachev (March 2, 1931 - August 30, 2022) was a Soviet politician. He was General Secretary of the Central Committee of the Communist Party of the Soviet Union from March 1985 to August 1991 and the last President of the Soviet Union from March 1990 to December 1991. He set new accents in Soviet politics with glasnost (openness), a commitment to freedom of expression, and perestroika (reconstruction), especially with the abolition of the planned economy. In disarmament negotiations with the USA, he initiated the end of the Cold War. He received the Nobel Peace Prize in 1990.

40) The Cold War is the conflict between the Western powers, led by the United States of America, and the so-called Eastern Bloc, led by the Soviet Union, which they fought with almost all means possible from 1947 to 1989. There was never a direct military conflict between the superpowers USA, the Soviet Union and their respective military blocs, although there were proxy wars such as the Korean War, the Vietnam War and the war in Afghanistan. The Cold War emerged as a systemic confrontation between capitalism and communism and determined foreign and security policy worldwide in the second half of the 20th century. For decades, political, economic, technical and military efforts were made on both sides to contain or push back the influence of the other camp worldwide.

41) Robert Ryan (November 11, 1909 - July 11, 1973) was an American actor. Ryan was busy in American film from the late 1940s until his death, appearing in many genres.

42) The Emmy Award, simply the Emmy, is the most important television award in the United States and - alongside the Academy Award (Oscar) for film, the Tony Award for theater and the Grammy Award for music - one of the four major American awards entertainment industry. It has been awarded annually since 1949 for the past television season in over 90 different categories.

43) Bob Ross: Happy Accidents, Betrayal & Greed (Bob Ross: Happy Accidents, Betrayal & Greed, USA 2021, 92 minutes, director: Joshua Rofé). Netflix documentary.

44) See 43).

45) https://www.artsy.net/article/artsy-editorial-bob-ross-owes-happy-trees-forgotten-painter (Accessed on November 22, 2023). 40) The Cold War is the conflict between the Western powers, led by the United States of America, and the so-called Eastern Bloc, led by the Soviet Union, which they fought with almost all means possible from 1947 to 1989. There was never a direct military conflict between the superpowers USA, the Soviet Union and their respective military blocs, although there were proxy wars such as the Korean War, the Vietnam War and the war in Afghanistan. The Cold War emerged as a systemic confrontation between capitalism and communism and determined foreign and security policy worldwide in the second half of the 20th century. For decades, political, economic, technical and military efforts were made on both sides to contain or push back the influence of the other camp worldwide.

46) https://www.youtube.com/watch?v=WiM2iiT7lBo (accessed on December 18, 2023).

47) https://www.artsy.net/article/artsy-editorial-bob-ross-owes-happy-trees-forgotten-painter (accessed on November 22, 2023).

48) See 43).

49) NY Times, December 22, 1991, page 33: „Bob Ross, the Frugal Gourmet of Painting."

50) See 49)

51) There is film footage of William on this fishing boat, driving it near the shore in calm weather and also lying at anchor. The shape of the boat looks something like a trawler, but the scale has been drastically reduced. In one scene, William moves in the open stern area, an almost bizarre-looking image (see photo on the right), because William is far too big in relation to the boat, and you can see how unstable it is, with every movement it wobbles. It would be in rough seas certainly capsized immediately. https://www.youtube.com/watch?v=OKEPISAof4E (Accessed on December 18, 2023).

52) Nanaimo in British Columbia is the second largest city on the Canadian Pacific island of Vancouver Island with around 90,000 inhabitants. The city is on the east side of the island. century. In technical language today we tend to talk about modern art.

53) „The Bill Alexander Story: An Autobiography." ISBN:0-8403-2990-3.

54) Pablo Ruiz Picasso (October 25, 1881 - April 8, 1973) was a Spanish painter, graphic artist and sculptor. His extensive oeuvre includes paintings, drawings, graphics, collages, sculptures and ceramics, the total number of which is estimated at 50,000. It is characterized by a wide variety of artistic expressions and techniques. The works from his Blue and Pink Periods, and the founding of Cubism together with Georges Braque, mark the beginning of his extraordinary artistic career.

55) Modern art, also known as modern art, is a relatively vague but commonly used term for the avant-garde art of the 20th century.

56) Charles Marion Russell (March 19, 1864 – October 25, 1926) was an American painter, sculptor, illustrator and writer. He became known for his depiction of the American West and created a total of more than 4,000 paintings and sculptures.

57) Political allegory is a narrative form in which meaning is conveyed through reference is constituted on a second level of meaning. Here the viewer has to make a transfer in

order to be able to interpret the content statements. What is crucial for the functioning of allegories is the viewer's awareness that, on the one hand, there are two language or image levels and, on the other hand, that allegories are ultimately oriented and designed for a specific goal.

58) George Grosz (July 26, 1893 to July 6, 1959) was a German-American painter, graphic artist, cartoonist and war opponent. George Grosz's socially and socially critical verist paintings and drawings, most of which were created in the 1920s, are attributed to the New Objectivity. These works are characterized by sometimes drastic and provocative depictions and often by political statements. But his work also has expressionist, dadaist and futurist features. Typical subjects are the big city, its strangeness (murder, perversion, violence) and the class differences that emerge in it. In his works, often caricatures, he mocks the ruling circles of the Weimar Republic, addresses social contrasts and particularly criticizes the economy, politics, the military and the clergy.

59) Emil Nolde (August 7, 1867 to April 13, 1956) was one of the leading Expressionist painters. He is one of the great watercolorists in 20th century art and is known for his expressive choice of colors.

60) David Alfaro Siqueiros (December 29, 1896 - January 6, 1974) was a Mexican painter, graphic artist, soldier during the Mexican Revolution and assassin. He is one of the main representatives of muralismo and, alongside José Clemente Orozco and Diego Rivera, belongs to the so-called Los Tres Grandes ("The Big Three"). As a supporter of Stalinism, he led a conspiracy to assassinate Leo Trotsky in 1940.

61) José Clemente Orozco (born November 23, 1883 to September 7, 1949) is considered the founder of contemporary Mexican painting. He is one of the main representatives of muralism and belongs to David Alfaro Siqueiros and Diego Rivera so-called Los Tres Grandes ("The Big Three").

62) Diego Rivera (December 8 or December 13, 1886 to November 24, 1957) was a Mexican painter. Along with David Alfaro Siqueiros and José Clemente Orozco, he is considered the most important modern painter in Mexico. From 1907 to 1921, Diego Rivera worked in Europe and in the United States at the beginning and end of the 1930s. In his panel paintings, Rivera quickly adapted many different styles and worked with Cubism for a long time. During his time in Europe he was in contact with leading representatives of modern art such as Picasso, Braque and Gris. After his return to Mexico, Diego Rivera worked primarily on his large mural projects, for example in the Palacio Nacional, the Palacio de Bellas Artes, the Secretaría de Educación Pública and in various institutions in the United States. These murals, which he saw as a contribution to popular education, contributed a large part to Rivera's fame and success.

63) "The Bill Alexander Story: An Autobiography." ISBN:0-8403-2990-3. S.227 ff.

64) Buonamico Buffalmacco (active around 1315–1336), was an important Italian painter of the Renaissance.

65) Naicam is a small town in rural Saskatchewan, around 220 km from the provincial capital Regina. The name of the town is a combination of the names of the railroad contractors "Naismith" and "Cameron."

These non-fiction books have also been published by Jörg-Michael Müller in recent years:

Nazis sentenced to death war criminals and theirs requests for clemency verbatim: documentation

Volume 1 - Paperback - March 31, 2022

Der aus Lübeck stammende Künstler und Autor Jörg-Michael Müller betreibt seit 2010 ein Atelier in Norddeutschland und erstellt Gemälde, Illustrationen und Objektkunst. Zu seinem vielschichtigen Spektrum gehören außerdem auch zahlreiche Publikationen rund um die Themen Kunst und Geschichte.

The pleas for clemency from the merciless: After their death sentences were announced, numerous Nazi war criminals submitted one in the hope of being able to avoid hanging. Written by hand, or formulated and submitted by family members or their defenders - some have already been documented verbatim, many have so far been forgotten or lost in the archives. As part of this documentation, the systematic and still incomplete search for these documents is carried out. Volume 1 starts with a series of selected requests for clemency from the most famous Nazi war criminals. You can also find out everything about the search for traces of the missing pleas for clemency from the first Bergen-Belsen trial in 1945, and read the verbatim arguments in mitigation presented in court for the "Belsen Gang" who were sentenced to death. Nazi war criminals sentenced to death and their REQUESTS FOR MERCY verbatim.

Defendant No. 9 - The "Hyena of Auschwitz" under cross-examination. The protocol. Expanded NEW EDITION: Over 70 historical documents, manuscripts and unpublished images

Paperback – September 1, 2021

Previously unpublished and spectacular archive material is here for the first time been brought together. Last photos and unique manuscripts found in an Canadian archive.

The concentration camp guard Irma Grese was the youngest war criminal who was sentenced to death by hanging in the Bergen-Belsen trial in 1945. She in particular attracted worldwide attention because the crimes she was accused of, the brutality and cruelty, and her sadism towards the prisoners were in stark contrast to her appearance. She had many names: "Hyena of Auschwitz," "Hell's Angel," or "Queen of Belsen." And her accuser said of her at the trial: "And there is not a single atrocity that took place in this camp for which she is not considered the person responsible was known. She regularly took part in the selection for the gas chamber, punished arbitrarily, and when she came to Belsen, she continued in exactly the same way." In this documentary we go on a search for clues in old files and archives and shed light on the 243 days of the year 1945 , from the liberation of the Bergen-Belsen concentration camp to the execution of the perpetrators in Hameln. We accompany Grese through the entire trial up to the gallows, look at the witness statements, read what the press wrote, discover little or hardly known things, correct errors and dive directly into the events when we question and cross-examine the defendants Follow No. 9. The language of this book is German.

Defendant No. 9: The "Hyena of Auschwitz" under cross-examination

Paperback – October 1, 2020

The concentration camp guard Irma Grese was the youngest war criminal who was sentenced to death by hanging in the Bergen-Belsen trial in 1945. She in particular attracted worldwide attention because the crimes she was accused of, the brutality and cruelty, and her sadism towards the prisoners were in stark contrast to her appearance. She had many names: "Hyena of Auschwitz," "Hell's Angel," or "Queen of Belsen." And her accuser said of her at the trial: "And there is not a single atrocity that took place in this camp for which she was not known to be responsible. She regularly took part in the selection for the gas chamber, punished arbitrarily, and when she came to Belsen, she continued in exactly the same way." In this documentary we go on a search for clues in old files and archives and shed light on the 243 days of the year 1945 , from the liberation of the Bergen-Belsen concentration camp to the execution of the perpetrators in Hamelin. We accompany Grese through the entire trial up to the gallows, look at the witness statements, read what the press wrote, discover little or hardly known things, correct errors and dive directly into the events when we question and cross-examine the defendants Follow No. 9. The language of this book is German.

J.M. Müller

Angeklagte Nr.9

Die „Hyäne von Auschwitz"
im Kreuzverhör. Das Protokoll.

Jörg-Michael Müller, sometimes magical, and sometimes satirical...

Jörg-Michael Müller's trimagic silver spell: Three magical visual effects
Paperback – January 24, 2022

Several months of development work were necessary for this extraordinary magical trick principle, with which truly fairytale-like and extremely powerful visual effects are possible. In this magic seminar booklet I present three wonderful magical effects: No complicated moves are necessary, no long rehearsals. The text is in German.

150 brilliantly absurd questions that the world has been waiting for!
Paperback – December 9, 2020

This volume contains countless witty, ironic, absurd, satirical and funny questions, enriched with humorous illustrations and inviting you to laugh, smile and ponder. Sitting bored in endless conferences is pure hard work when you're trying not to fall asleep. I tend to compensate for this ever- simmering boredom at my newspaper conferences by starting to doodle with my pen and only letting fragments of the collective drivel penetrate me, which then mutate into bizarre questions In the end I would rather leave it unsaid. Some of these hard-earned results now seem to me to be ready for humanity.
The text is in German.